BRANCHES

ON THE

CONEJO

REVISITED

By

Anne Schroeder

Branches on the Conejo Revisited
Revised 2nd edition October, 2020.
Published ©2020 Anne Schroeder
www.anneschroederauthor.com

ISBN 978-1-7348684-2-5

Previous edition by RD&C Publishers, Nov 2001.

Book cover: RossanoDesigns, RossanoDesgins.weebly.com

All photographs used with permission

Poem written for Caspar Borchard Sr.
by his granddaughter, Hazel Penny,
On the occasion of his 86th birthday, 1928.

Caspar Borchard Senior,
You who have been so brave and true,
Came sailing the deep blue ocean
In a sail boat made for two.

Some sixty years ago you started
To sail o'er life's great way,
After nine months of brave struggling,
You landed in the U.S.A.

You have worked with untiring efforts
And courage to steer things along;
Then we all came over to greet you
And help to gladden the song.

We have been so happy, grandfather,
Improving this land of ours,
To know you were our founder
In the land of beautiful flowers.

You always have stood by us
With comfort and with care,
And unkind words from you
Have been a thing so rare.

So on your eighty-sixth birthday,
We all have been longing to see,
Your dear face smiling and happy,
And many fine wishes for thee.

"From you, I only ask respect/Do not lay your story over mine."

—— La Reina, the Burro Lady of Far West Texas
Excerpted from *We Make a Small Herd* by Lucy Griffith

TABLE OF CONTENTS

INTRODUCTION

History has always been a very fascinating subject to me. I am always intrigued by the way it opens windows into the past, providing glimpses of what life used to be like, relaying the trials and tribulations people faced and giving us a keener sense of our own heritage. Looking back through time often gives us a clearer picture of who we are and where we came from. It can be even more enlightening when we have a personal connection to the history of a particular place or people. Such is the case for my affinity to the Conejo Valley.

My grandfather, Joel McCrea, who was born in 1905, got his first glimpse of the Conejo Valley in 1916. He was ten years old and driving through with his family on their way to the Pan-Pacific Expo/World's Fair in San Francisco. He would later recall to me how he remembered the beauty of the rolling hills and the oak trees as they traveled by. It would almost seem as though there was some sort of divine intervention in that some 17 years later when looking to purchase a ranch he would once again be drawn back to the valley he had seen as a young boy.

He purchased the first portion of his home ranch in the spring of 1933. He married my grandmother, actress Frances Dee, in the fall of that same year and together they began to settle into their rural lifestyle and raise a family. My grandparents were both actors and most folks in those days recognized them from the many movies they made. But my grandfather's boyhood dream was to be a rancher and he always considered acting as a means to help achieve his ranching aspirations. He always loved the outdoors and especially enjoyed working with animals. The ranch stretched from the head of the Santa Rosa Valley, where he built his headquarters, south into the Conejo Valley where the bulk of the acreage stretched forth. During its heyday the ranch consisted of just shy of 2,400 acres. Little did they know in 1933 how entwined they would become with the people and the places of the Conejo Valley.

In the beginning my grandfather was a bit of a novice at the ranching business but he never wanted to be considered a "gentleman rancher". In fact, even during the height of his acting career, he always listed "rancher" as his occupation on his tax return and acting as a hobby. He was always eager to learn and become a better steward of the land and his neighboring farmers and ranchers were always willing to share their experience and knowledge. Folks like the Olsens, the Pedersons, the Borchards and the Kelleys were quick to provide advice when needed. Often times my grandfather would be invited to help work cattle at other ranches in the vicinity like the Stratherns in Simi Valley or the Hearst ranch in what is now Westlake. He was always "hands on" with all the activities at the ranch and quickly became very respected among his neighbors as a hard working, knowledgeable cattleman and farmer. At the same time, my grandmother was given much insight into the role of a rancher's wife from the other wives in the area! While she took most of that advice to heart, some of it she would later recall with a hearty laugh! Together, my grandparents became an integral part of the community and were proud to do so. They were always willing to lend a helping hand when needed.

My grandparents taught their three boys the value of hard work and instilled in them a respect for the land and the people that worked it. It was a great way to grow up and there were lots of lively stories that come out of those times as kids growing up in the country! Those life lessons have continued to be passed down over the years.

After four generations of my family being in the Conejo Valley I am proud to say that many of those relationships and friendships that started back in 1933 continue to this day. I stay in touch with many of the relatives of some of the original families including members of the Olsen family, the Kelley family, the Borchard family and the Clark family – all names that are recounted in the pages that follow. Who would have ever guessed that those friendships nurtured decades ago would continue to exhibit themselves in different ways even to this day!

The majority of the old landmarks of the area are long gone but I am proud to say that the core of the old McCrea Ranch – all the barns, the bunkhouse (the first building on the ranch built in 1890), and the main house (built in 1933) - all continue to live on today. The ranch is now listed on the National Register of Historic Places and we also have a special plaque in the parking lot that pays homage to the Norwegian farmers who built the Norwegian Grade (Moorpark Road) that cuts through the ranch. You can learn more about the history of the ranch by visiting – www.mccrearanchfoundation.org

I am grateful to Anne Schroeder for taking on the task of putting this book together and for sharing all of the history it presents. I am also appreciative for her allowing me to be a small part of it!

Above all, I am most grateful to the descendents of the Norwegian Colony families who were so helpful and made my grandparents feel so welcome back in 1933! As my grandfather once said of the Conejo Valley "...I met some of the most wonderful people I ever knew. It was home. I am filled with gratitude for my memories of the integrity of the old-timers of the area and I hope... we can honor our past and make a promise to the future."

Wyatt McCrea, President, McCrea Ranch Foundation – www.mccrearanchfoundation.org

Rodeo on the Gillibrand Ranch, 1920

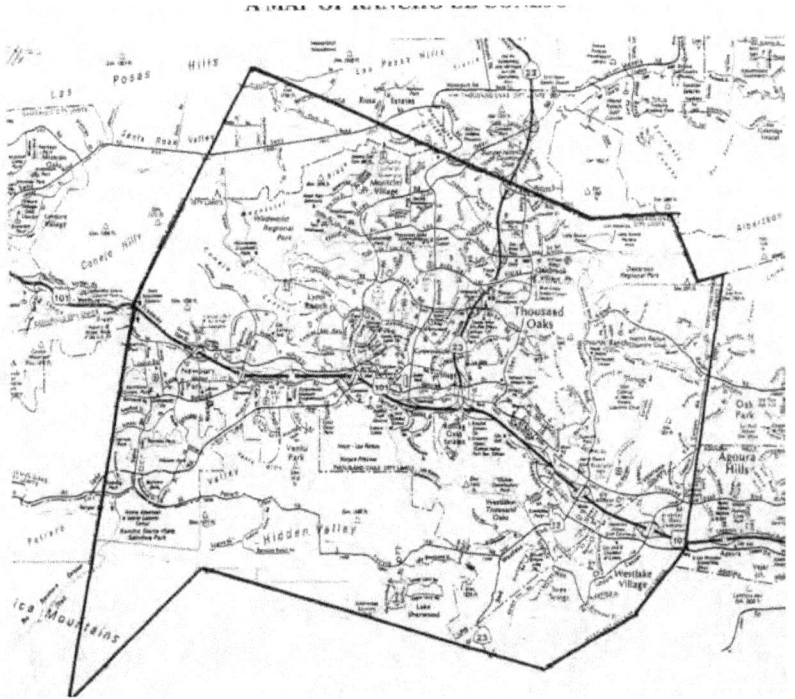

El Conejo Map

Norwegian Colony

CHAPTER ONE

Sweet Partings

THE IDEA FOR this book began one morning when my mother phoned. "I'm the last one left," she said. "We had 160 members of the Olsen/Borchard families and I'm the oldest one left." For eight decades she observed life with an artist's eye and an empathic heart for the sorrows and misfortunes of others. I heard in her voice the unspoken fear that when she died the stories would die with her. I remember shutting down the screen of my computer where I was working on a novel and taking a firmer grip on the phone.

"Tell me the stories again Mom, and this time I'll listen." I picked up a notebook and a fresh pen. "Start anywhere, Mom. I'm ready."

Her younger sister Mary had spent decades collecting, researching and collating our family history. It was the human stories—the immeasurable anecdotes Mom had heard and experienced that disturbed her sleep and fretted her later years. She felt a responsibility to pass them forward as surely as she did her Norwegian grandmother's wedding trunk. But as happens with memory, recollections vary. I used much of Mary Rydberg's research, without which this book would not be possible. True historians may object to my adding creative elements, but as Mark Twain said, "Never let the truth get in the way of a good story." When I placed the first copy into my mother's hands she clasped it to her breast, bowed her head and whispered; "Now I can die." Jean Olsen Thompson passed in late 2017, at 92.

My grandparents, Oscar and Theresa Olsen, lived in a world where events passed in slow, measured cadence. They were predictable, comfortable people whose lives evolved slowly enough that grandchildren shared the same experiences. Orange sherbet served in glass bowls on Friday evenings. Television with only one channel. The feel and scent of starched sheets on the guest bed. The spit and polish of an air-tight De Soto sedan—the stuff of memories.

Before she died Theresa was simply 'Grandma.' For this book she is 'Tracy,' the nickname her sisters and brothers used for her. 'Grandma' belongs in my memories.

Fourteen years after her passing I was still haunted by her loss. We were blessed with a long and close relationship. Why then did her death at 86 leave me so bereft? Why, many years later, do I still miss her? It was in the course of writing that I came to realize the roots of my sorrow. I grieved for my grandmother of course, but in a larger sense I mourned the loss of an era, of innocence, of all that was and can no longer be; a time when life unfolded with such freshness and wonder that it molded the psyches of a later generation. What disappeared with Tracy's passing represents the very best of rural America. She stood as an icon to practicality, perseverance and grit. She saw her duty and she fulfilled it clearly and simply.

Oscar was a Renaissance man, a free thinker. Fiercely pragmatic, steadfast in his beliefs, he was a man whose lifetime spanned the apex of American farming. Seldom before retirement did he leave his farm for any length of time—occasional jobs to supplemented his family, and once to spend two weeks on a jury trial in Ventura. He was a trustee for the Pleasant Valley School Board, a civil servant with Ventura County, a man whose farm implements and family photographs are displayed in the Stagecoach Inn Museum in Newbury Park, the heart of his beloved Conejo (cone-ay-ho, Spanish for 'rabbit') Valley.

Like his father Nils, he was a talented machinist and furniture maker. Both lived their lives believing in the dignity of all men. Their progeny have cause to be proud of the stubborn Norwegian blood that courses through our veins. Ours is the practical, hard-working legacy of plain-faced European immigrants who built America, and their own futures, one task at a time. Their lives encapsulated an era of Southern California. Perhaps, by sharing their memories and stories, I have done my duty.

In her final years, the trees Tracy planted as a new bride stood her vigil in the early mornings while the first buds of the cottonwood brushed against the naked windowsill. The wind became her ally in the way it scraped and worried the brittle winter branches against the clapboard siding of the farmhouse. The harsh energy of the northwest wind vented the emotions that filled her. She spoke of none of this, but I saw her eyes glisten as she fought to control the last vestiges of her destiny. She was my mother's mother, Theresa Kelley Olsen. Tracy to her friends—Grandma.

I am her namesake. I learned her ways in unspoken parody, shared her thoughts over innumerable mugs of milk tea and cookies. In her last days I saw the torment that clouded her gray eyes.

As she lay in a hospital bed in Los Angeles, far from her farmhouse, it was the trees that captured her essence, ancient elms and cottonwoods that shattered the stark sunlight into a canopy of lace, a whisper of light upon raging conflict. In her last days she wavered between consciousness and respite. Watching her, I learned that death is summoned when the will to live grows weary. When Tracy's fierce hold on life ebbed, her mind accepted eternity as her destiny. She did not invite death into herself as much as she allowed life to leave.

Our family is not one to store its mourning clothes in the back closet. We show our respect up front and personal. In the weeks and days when waiting was all we could do, her grandchildren spelled our mothers and aunts at Tracy's bedside, our sense of place akin to holding a second trust deed on a house about to be repossessed. The older generation held the first claim. They relayed the doctor's information and we waited to be told the news. When the time came for final good-byes I found myself unable to face the task alone. Tracy laid so still, so pliant, little more than a pile of bedclothes arranged against a blue waffle-weave hospital blanket. A plastic chair stood at the foot of her bed but I ignored it. I had not made my journey to sit so far from her side.

I shared my visit with a brother and a cousin, quiet farmers whose sadness crowded the room as they hung back at the door and masked their grief in mute misery. My throat choked with the rawness of farewell. My reason for coming had been simple; I thought I could bear to let her go if I could only hold her hand once more. I leaned close and whispered while I stroked her fingers, brushed them against my cheek. I felt her pulse, so faint, so patient, as though she was waiting for each of us to say goodbye. *What must she be thinking?* I wondered. *What must she be thinking?*

As though she read my thoughts, Tracy opened her eyes, her weary smile conveying pleasure that we had come. I felt blessed to find her awake; had been warned to expect otherwise. Seeing her so still, so helpless, seemed to punch the air from my diaphragm. When I could breathe again, loneliness filled the space in my lungs. She wasn't even gone and already I felt the bleakness of her loss. I swallowed the lump in my throat and returned her smile. She seemed to be waiting to speak. I made up my mind not to tire her, but the words slipped out one by one.

Like old times we chatted, the two of us, alone almost. Her mind remained keen to the last. Leaning into the bed, I reminded her of the lessons she had taught us, named a dozen trips we had shared, reminisced of summers at her beach cabin. Had my mother been present she would have thought our conversation odd. She might have cautioned me not to tire Grandma.

My words continued, weighed against the fear in her eyes. Never one to suffer tears, that day, Tracy fretted for her judgment, for the time when God would tally the product of her life. "It doesn't hurt now," she said. "I just make a lot of noise." So undignified these words on a deathbed that we both laughed.

Smiling, I turned to see the grave faces of the two men behind me, imagined their throats with lumps they couldn't swallow. A spokes-grandchild, I wanted to say something for each of us. "You've taught us how to live; now you're teaching us how to die."

"I hope so," With the quiet words, she ceased fidgeting her arthritic fingers against the waffle weave blanket and turned her face to mine. While eternity waited behind the wisdom of her eyes, I held her gaze and prayed that Heaven would be the place where we would next meet.

A sudden flash of panic in her eyes betrayed a fear too strong to dismiss. I wanted to tell her there was nothing to fear, but perhaps such blasphemy to a dying woman would be the greatest sin of all. In silence, I promised that I would pray for her, would hold her close for all the days that separated us. I repeated the promise aloud so she would hear it. The storm left her eyes and serenity surrounded her like a mantle.

I wanted to weep for what I had stolen from my brother, my cousin; what I had seen in the depths of her eyes while they waited at the door. I wanted them to step closer, to hold her hand, to smooth her brow and feel the softness of her skin, but the distance from the door to her bedside was a journey neither could take. How terrible to be a man, that their tears should be cloaked behind their sadness.

Ashen faced, it was all they could do to lean against the wall and cast long glances at the floor. Their scattered gazes didn't rest long on Tracy. How good it was to be a woman, to let tears stream down my face and to let my words quiver when I couldn't finish a sentence. Never had I loved either of them more—my brother or my cousin—than on that day. Never had I loved Grandma more.

Her daughters arrived from a well-deserved coffee break, after spending hours at her bedside. "She didn't speak, did she? She's been in a coma for three days," my mother whispered.

I glanced at the farmers, but they left it to me whether I should admit the truth, to decide whether my admission would be too cruel. Turning back, Tracy had slipped back into her peaceful place. She didn't speak again.

How harsh that she would hide from her daughters, but such are the secrets that temper our lives. Perhaps I too will hide from my children when they confer with the doctor over my bedside and fret about whether the room is too warm. Tracy would have said that such issues between her and her daughters were just the imagination.

Life has taught me that sometimes children are a responsibility that arrives when we are trying to find our own fit in the fabric of life. It was so with my mother; it is so with me and my own children. As a granddaughter I remained unaware of any fractures in my grandmother's life. Her children might know otherwise, but to me, Tracy never seemed to make a misstep.

Fortune graced her with the perfect place to grow up, the Conejo Valley of Southern California during its heyday of rural seclusion. Fortune graced her with a birth in a centennial year and with a twin brother, John Louis. The fact that she was born in Talbert, California, was an accident of circumstance. Her parents, Rosa and Silas Kelley, were farming the flatlands near Huntington Beach when Tracy was born on November 19, 1900, in the midst of a hundred-year flood that cut short her father's farming venture and washed his topsoil into the Pacific Ocean.

The story Tracy told was that Silas had intended to summon the doctor, but the rains started and the road became impassible for the doctor's spring buggy. Silas managed to bring a midwife back on horseback to assist in the birth. His wife's labor pains continued into the night. In darkness he began boring a hole in the floor. When it was finished, he pushed his finger in as far as he could reach. "If I can feel water," he said, "We have to leave." He monitored the hole throughout the night, but never felt the rising water. Daylight came and the babies arrived. When the rains subsided in a day or two, the midwife left Rosa and her three children to wait out the winter.

By April, the adobe wagon ruts had dried to a passable sludge. Tracy and her twin were five months old and their brother Charlie, almost two, when Rosa loaded them into a wagon and drove the buckboard through the badlands of Calabasas. Silas rode with them to the Ventura County line, to protect them from highwaymen before turning back alone.

Rosa returned to her father's home, arranged for the baptisms of her babies and never left the valley again for any extended period. Silas returned a few months later after harvesting his summer crops. He eventually built a house on a parcel of land in the Conejo located near his father's land.

Two more sons were born, one 15 months after the other so that Rosa had five children under the age of six—four boisterous boys and one girl. It was rumored that Rosa's strapping brothers paid a visit to her husband that quelled the idea of more babies in the immediate future. True or not, it was well over a decade before another girl arrived—and two more after that. Genetically, the blend of Irish and German proved to be a good match. All the babies lived. Tracy grew up with four feisty brothers who teased her unmercifully and wore their mother out trying to keep them safe and occupied. Left with only boys for company, Tracy learned to drive a buggy, saddle her horse and ride with a man's ease.

Theresa at age 12 rode with a man's ease.

She also learned at a very young age that a disproportionate amount of work fell to a female. Her mother was worn out with the toils of motherhood that included scratch cooking, tending chickens and garden, mending and washing clothing. Tracy was expected to work inside while her brothers rode horses and tended livestock.

Still, there was time for recreation. The tempo of her life maintained an assurance that there would be time for everything she wanted to do. The grain fields outside her father's door provided a rhythm that varied only with the seasons. Tracy planted trees with the possibility that she would still be living in the same house when they matured.

———————

During the 1950s, the last decade of simplicity, Tracy taught lessons that have served me well. In a woman's youth, if she is lucky, she learns who she is not. Through the early decades of adulthood she strives to become the person she wants to be. By the time she reaches 50, she has time to embrace life's possibilities. As grandchildren arrive, a woman should be nothing less than what her destiny requires. A woman should live her life so that her grandchildren will learn from her. These are the lessons Tracy taught me. Now that I have grandchildren, I teach them the same.

I was 38 the year Tracy died, old and young at the same time. My daughter was eighteen. I looked at her and thought how young she was, devoid of wisdom over things that matter in life, such as glimpsing death waiting behind clouded eyes. When our matriarch passed, adjustments rippled though the bloodline. Daughters took mother's place. Lives took on moral imperative. Memories were revisited, formed, categorized and saved in the broken places that remained. With Tracy's passing, new vitality flowed into the rootstock; new branches sprang from old trunks.

Strange, the things I missed with the death of a grandmother—the things I connected with her in the hope that life could be the same again. Often, the keepsake we claim for ourselves would make no sense to anyone else. My childhood memories were embodied in an old clock I found setting on her nightstand the week of her funeral. The alarm on Tracy's Baby Ben clock no longer rang, nor did the hands move when I carefully picked it up the way she showed me as a child. For years it sat on her night table, cozened up against flattened tubes of Ben-Gay and her worn rosary beads. I used to play with it, fit its brass key into the four-sided stem and wind it clockwise until the spring was too stiff to turn. "Don't over-wind," she would warn.

Her words seemed to link us as I sat on her double bed and tried to remember the way things used to be. Long ago, when the clock ticked, I'd watch to see if the key turned, but it was like trying to watch the moon crawling across the night sky. Settings could be adjusted on the back of the clock with tiny brass fittings marked with capital letters. 'Loud' and 'Soft.' I used to set off the alarm by jangling the twin domes with my finger while she vacuumed the floor with her ancient Electrolux, its frayed cord mended with electrical tape and its flannel bag mended on her ancient Singer sewing machine.

The last time I wound it, the clock stopped working. Someone gave her a radio alarm clock for Christmas, but she left the broken Baby Ben on her night table.

The night I stepped into her room, I held the clock to my ear and tried to coax a *tick* from its worn-out innards. I thought about slipping the useless clock into my pocket, but that would nullify the trust our family held in each other. Instead, I rested my face on her pillow and smelled her talc and liniment. For a minute she was still there and I was a child again.

Tracy's funeral was celebrated with jubilation. She had gone to her Father and no longer suffered the agony of worn joints that had kept her confined to a wheelchair for a decade. The funeral Mass was held in Oxnard's Santa Clara Catholic Church, with its beautiful domed ceilings and frescos nearly as old as Tracy herself. The church exuded a serenity that belonged to another time, 1904, when European immigrants built the church with the help of master craftsmen and imported Italian marble statues.

I arrived early for the service, wearing a crème-colored dress because I refused to wear black. Alone in the quiet church I allowed my mind to associate events of her life. She would have enjoyed the service in the small domed church that smelled of beeswax and musty wood—the church where she had made her First Communion. Her funeral did not provide the solace I sought. I waited for a feeling of letting go, of saying good-bye that never came. A priest who had never known her gave the eulogy, skimming the highpoints of her life without touching her essence, like a book reviewed by someone who had only seen the movie.

Tracy had issues with her religion—more to do with practicality than matters of faith. She lived in an era when, in order to take Communion on Sunday, the faithful were obliged to attend Saturday Confession. In the middle of the day, when the garden needed harvesting and she was steamy from canning, she would tussle with her spiritual conscience. If she didn't travel the seven miles to four o'clock Confession, she might have to sit alone in the pew at Communion the next morning while the rest of the congregation partook. She made the trip usually twice a year, at Easter and Christmas. As she was fond of saying, if any priest had cared to visit, he would see that a farmwife's daily chores were penance enough for any sins she might have committed.

Funerals for Tracy's Conejo relatives, the Borchards, were highly anticipated events that provided children with a sense of the natural order of life's cycle. I attended six such funerals before I reached my twelfth birthday. They left an indelible impression. I learned that lasting virtue lies in living a practical, frugal, hardworking life.

I learned that having wealth lends glory to the departed. Funerals involved elegant caskets, incense, and elaborate arrangements that surpassed the old-fashioned flowers grown in home gardens like we were used to. The Borchards were wealthy people; their funerals were significant events. The "Orange County" Borchard sisters and brothers arrived in expensive automobiles and funeral limousines, but they dressed in the same serge dresses and suits for each event they attended. They did not buy new outfits to bury their dead.

Tracy's aunts and uncles were ancient men and women whose children and grandchildren filled half the rows in St. Mary Magdalen Catholic Church in Camarillo. The names of these Borchard elders were as familiar as the Yankees lineup might be to a group of children playing stickball in the streets of New York City. *FrankCharlesLeoCasparAntone MaryRosaTeresa*; my sisters and I would race through the list on our way to each funeral, reviewing their names, and those of their spouses, before we stood on tiptoes to peek at the deceased in the casket, their waxen cheeks painted the false blush of death. Glorious.

Hothouse carnations and roses surrounded Tracy's casket, but it was her Brazilian pepper tree that evoked memories. The peace of her farmhouse evenings filled me as I revisited them inside the church that day. The priest blessed the casket and sprinkled it with holy water. He returned to the altar, retrieved a smoking incense burner suspended from a long, golden chain; rocked it from side-to-side, wafting incense into the room while languor stole through me.

I recalled sitting next to Tracy on Sundays, she dressed like the Queen Mother in her white gloves and stiff black hat, and I trying not to twitch when the sermon ran long. *She would enjoy the service*, I thought on the day of her funeral. She had waited a long time to be reunited in death with her beloved husband, Oscar.

CHAPTER TWO

Tracy's House

WHENEVER MY MOTHER allowed me to spend the weekend at Tracy's, the experience seemed sweeter than heaven. Once every few weeks my mother would load her ever-expanding brood of children and prerequisite diapers and bottles to make the nine-mile trip to Tracy's and Oscar's—a 20-minute drive over sloping knolls along Moorpark Road to the end of Olsen Road. For small children, riding in the back seat of a sedan, most of the passing scenery was glimpsed as sky and pepper trees from the low back seat of a sedan, the route memorized from bumps and curves in the road by children who couldn't see out of the small rounded side window ports. When we were almost there, we eagerly watched for the road sign at the corner announcing 'Olsen Road,' named for my grandfather's people. The car rolled past the Pedersons' orchards laden with the scent of citrus, past the "old home place" farm where the McAfees now lived, past the white farmhouse at Pederson Corner. When we reached the grove of towering blue gum eucalyptus, we knew we'd arrived.

Following tea and cake, we were excused to follow the woodlands and the creek as far as the barbwire fence at the edge of the Janss Ranch. We climbed the hayloft, rode the pulley ropes to the ground and frightened the penned sheep until they ran in circles, blatting. Once, we climbed the rickety ladder to poke at a sleeping barn owl. In the aftermath of Tracy's lecture we girls lost our daring, but our older brother Mel continued to climb the ladder long afterward.

With the sun low in the west, Tracy and my mother would stroll toward our beige Studebaker with a bouquet of newspaper-wrapped hollyhocks or irises, or a sack of oranges. It was time to leave. If it was Saturday, and if Tracy was planning to attend church at the Acorn Theater where we held Mass on Sunday, I was occasionally permitted to spend the night. I would stand beside my grandmother while my family drove off, my heart beating to the rhythm of my thoughts; *my turn . . . my turn*. As soon as the Studebaker rounded the eucalyptus grove, Tracy was mine. But there were rules to be obeyed.

We waved my family off and returned to the house. I washed my hands and face in the bathroom before setting the table with an efficiency that would have surprised my mother. Supper meant chicken soup with thick homemade noodles, plain soda crackers with store-bought butter, and Knudsen cottage cheese straight from the yellow and white carton. Tracy served it with her own canned cling peaches spooned from a quart Mason jar.

The evening routine rarely varied. Grandpa would scan the *National Geographic* or *Farm Journal* while Tracy read the *Ventura Star Free Press*. At seven o'clock, I'd dish orange sherbet into three carnival glass dishes, careful that Grandpa got the largest serving. With my stocking feet tucked beneath me, I'd sit in a Queen Anne chair and nibble mouse-bites while eucalyptus crackled in the woodstove and the black and white television offered up a fuzzy half-hour episode of "Beat the Clock."

It was always "Tracy's house," even though Oscar began building it before their marriage. They chose a house from a catalogue and had it shipped in on the train and hired a carpenter to complete it in the weeks following their wedding in 1921. The house was a clapboard single-story farmhouse with two bedrooms and a long bathroom that opened to the outside so grubby workmen didn't have to traipse through the house to use the facilities. It was built with an open porch, perfect for the hanging swing that graced one corner.

By the time grandchildren arrived, the house had been enlarged and the porch enclosed to include two additional bedrooms. Its space seemed infinite in the way everything seems grand and palatial in childhood, with secret crannies and shadowy corners where the dim wattage from two table lamps barely seemed to penetrate the gloom. The original 230 volt fuse panel allowed for a 20 amp kitchen circuit and three 15-amp lighting circuits that included a single plug-in for each room. With small wattage bulbs in the two permissible lamps, rooms seemed perpetually dark. At the end of the living room, a pair of built-in china cabinets bookended a storage chest with a recessed finger-pull. On rare occasions we were allowed to open the lid to view an old Norwegian fiddle and a wooden flute that lay among other relics of seemingly reverent and taboo nature.

At the end of the hall stood an ancient pump organ, brought over from Germany on a long-ago schooner. It was given to Tracy as an early wedding gift, but at the time the bellows were broken. A cousin arranged for a craftsman to pick it up for repairs; Tracy had no recourse when months passed without word from the repairman. About 20 years later, a stranger drove up and unloaded an ornate organ from the back of an old truck. It was Tracy's with the bellows repaired. But the driver had no explanation for where it had been all those years. Oscar built an alcove at the end of the hallway to house it and the grandchildren were allowed to carefully pump the bellows and play the chords.

Tracy's valuables were displayed in cherrywood cabinets in her narrow dining room. The shelves were filled with silver, crystal and china dishes—dime-store pretties stacked alongside heirlooms brought over from the 'old country,' by German or Norwegian relatives. Each was precious because of post-war scarcity. She especially cherished a set of Art Deco candleholders, a wedding gift from Eleanor and James Burke, vaudeville and screen actor-cousins and my mother, Eugenia Eleanor's, namesake.

A bedroom down the hall served as a guestroom. A luxurious double bed filled one end of the room, mounded with a white chenille bedspread and lofty down pillows with crisply starched pillowcases. Strangely, the room made the double-bed appear oversized rather than the other way around. A built-in bookshelf and writing desk lent a sophisticated literary appearance that a would-be writer could appreciate. The closet sported matching double doors that stuck together with the solidness of tight carpentry and multiple coats of enamel paint.

A row of recessed drawers behind them provided us with happy hours recreating the immensely popular *Mickey Mouse's Clubhouse*. We would settle our little brothers, sisters and cousins on the floor while one of the older kids built up the suspense, inching open the doors at a nerve-wracking pace that caused the audience of four and five year-olds to squirm and squeal. The hinges creaked. The sticking doors necessitated a tug as our audience chanted: "Meeska, mooska mousekateer, tell us the name to open here." With the room in a hypnotic grip, one of us older kids would reach into the drawer and pull out the envelope, just like on the real show. We would repeat the performance over and over until our young audience caught on that there was no cartoon forthcoming and abandoned the stage set for cookies in the kitchen.

Memories of Tracy inevitably involved some sort of task. She lived in the here-and-now, brusquely intent on keeping idle hands occupied. No philosopher; her life lessons came whenever she saw a need. She was not an easy taskmaster, neither prone to compliments nor easy assurances, never a hugger or a woman given to praise. Her sharpness was not to be taken personally; it was just her way as it had been her mother's. Grandchildren learned that the absence of criticism was proof of a job well done.

We were raised with an obligation to keep up her house and yard and we never doubted her right to our labor. By the age of eight we were expected to wield a hoe in the flowerbeds without chopping a seedling; to distinguish between pickled beets and crabapples—quart from pint— to fetch last year's remains off the canning shelf before starting on the new. "Put it on the counter," meant that we had plucked the right jar from the shelf or carrot from the garden. We learned that a warning was given only once. Mistakes held consequence—a bee sting for forgetting to wear shoes when we hung laundry; rattlesnakes in the flowerbeds if we didn't keep watch; lunch promptly at noon, whether the chores were finished or not. Tracy's reward came in the way she shared her world.

———

Oscar and Theresa in Moorpark with their new DeSoto

Living among the Norwegian Colony and her extended family made Tracy close-mouthed. After her death we cousins tried to piece together the quilt of her life, adding our stories like quilt swatches stitched together with laughter and amazement. It was strange, the parts of herself that she chose to share. Her life had remained constant for so many years. She died before the advent of rapid social change. I believe she didn't share details because she didn't think they would seem interesting.

My cousin recalls lunchtime at Tracy's kitchen table, Tracy flirting with Oscar, teasing him about her other beaus and seeing a flare of jealousy in his reaction to something they hadn't discussed in 55 years together. The stories of the Norwegian Colony were recalled and passed on to children and grandchildren until they became part of our own story, even the names of people who were not related. Oscar's sharing came mostly through our mothers. He was worn out when his last grandchildren came along. He had made peace with the past and placed his hopes and energies on the present. Grandchildren eased the hardships of his childhood and provided proof that our genetic line was healthy. He was happy to give us a two-bit coin for a good report card and have us stand on his shoe tips while he danced us around. Seeing his towheaded grandchildren playing brought him peace and satisfaction. He was introspective and often quiet as he grew older, apt to take up a hoe and help us clear our farm of goatshead while he told us stories about his childhood.

His lessons weren't monumental, but they were constant and reliable. When my shoelace came untied on a walk, he knelt in the dirt and taught me to tie it with a double knot. He explained the significance of last names, why mine was different from his, and coached me until I could spell Thompson without hesitation. He taught me the value of asking questions and imbued my life with curiosity and an eye to possibility.

In later years our grandparents' economy of praise became a common family trait. Caught between plain talk and New Education with its happy faces, gold stars and praise—however slightly earned—as parents of school-age children, some of us felt pressure to assume a style that did not sit well with our basic tenets. In those days a job done well was its own reward. Tracy was stingy with her praise, probably because she had never known any other way.

She required that her younger guests take a bath before bed so that the sheets could be used for the next guest. As a five-year-old, I'd dally until her bedtime warning turned hard- edged and I knew she meant it. She wasn't the tucking-in type of grandmother, but the bid-you-goodnight-in-the-living-room type, so I had to make the trek down the dark hall alone. Pausing at the door I'd gulp air, hit the light switch and make a flying leap. After gaining the mattress I'd hide under the covers until my pulse slowed and my eyelids grew heavy.

During the night, peacocks called from the trees and homely little guinea hens issued rude squawks from wherever they clustered. Coyotes howled from the Indian caves at the top of the bluff. Sometimes the hound dog sleeping beneath my window snarled and tore off down the path after a rabbit or fox. Tracy thought I was an easy sleeper because in the morning the bed was scarcely rumpled. Had she known about my night terrors she would have concluded that I was too young to stay alone.

One of the rooms in Tracy's house was inviolate. Uncle Neil's bedroom was empty because he was off at high school and later, college. As rooms went it was small and spare, with a desk, a single bed, a dresser and a closet. His bookshelves held a treasure-trove of adventures for small hands, including gaudy westerns with dog-eared covers from which swaggering, two-fisted heroes faced slant-eyed foes with guns blazing.

One afternoon I slipped into Neil's room and found a paperback with a picture of Red Ryder, rugged and slack-jawed, relaxing after a day of grueling western adventure. Behind Red, a window—amazingly similar to those in Tracy's guestroom—opened onto the night sky. A cougar crouched at the edge of the sill, poised to leap upon the unsuspecting Red Ryder, its face distorted in a feral scream that silenced the wind. Time and again I sneaked in to study that book, searching the pages of indecipherable print for some hint of Red Ryder's fate. My older brother Mel, seven and scarcely reading, wasn't much help. We studied the picture together and agreed that things looked grim for Red. There was no one I could ask. Tracy would have told me to shut the door and get away. My writer's imagination was born in that room, inventing scenarios to rescue Red Ryder from certain death.

In Tracy's house every item held a permanence that we failed to recognize at the time. Plastic was just making its post-war appearance. Her things were crafted of wood or leather, brass or thick glass. Oscar's paperweights, his magnifying glass, his fountain pens and ink jars were meant to last several lifetimes. In the manner of a woman who appreciated her belongings and the labor it had taken to earn them, Tracy kept a spotless house and filled it with items that served a purpose. Her leather chairs and ottoman had a weathered comfort born of hard use. Her carpets were area rugs, purchased after they could afford them. Her furniture smelled of lemon polish. For as long as she was able to grow them, she kept vases filled with fresh flowers from her garden. During winter the hearth held a burning log. On her kitchen table she kept an ancient canister filled with cookies, home-baked for most of her life, store-bought in her later years when arthritis inflamed her joints and twisted her fingers. She kept a favorite teapot, its faded gold rim and nicks familiar to everyone who ever sat at her table.

Oscar would come in from the field to snack on a cold pancake from the breadbox topped with a thin layer of jam. Sometimes family or neighbors would drop by to share stories and laugh while he sat hunched over his tea with his weathered farmer's fingers cupping his mug.

Tracy's parents had been coffee drinkers, as were the other Norwegians on the Colony, until WW II caused coffee beans to be rationed. Oscar got tired of shortages, dashed expectations and the nuisance of rationing coupons. He decided that his household would make the switch to black tea, which wasn't rationed. With the addition of their farm honey and cow's milk they found the flavor tolerable. When guests dropped by they were able to offer tea, hot or iced, and by the time the war ended they were used to the change and never went back.

During WW II, Oscar manned the Civil Air Patrol telephone a few miles away in Santa Rosa Valley. He and his neighbors took turns in pairs on around-the-clock shifts. The government phone was not to be used for personal reasons. Volunteers served in four-hour stints, sitting in a five-by-eight-foot shack at the Gerry Farm, their job to identify and report all aircraft that flew within their spotting area. Echo-Echo-Black was the code for that portion of the Conejo. For each shift, two spotters worked together; one called out the numbers painted on the bottom of a wing while the other manned the phone. Nick Olsen and Rich Pederson took part in the Civil Air Patrol airplane watch as well. Oscar and his daughter Jean shared shifts while she was in high school.

Their contribution to national security didn't end with the war. Through the years of the Cold War, Oscar kept his field glasses and an official flight manual near his back door. Whenever a plane flew overhead, we were instructed to maintain strict silence so he could concentrate. He took his duty seriously. His grandchildren thought that during the war he had single-handedly saved California from Japanese air attack. We didn't realize there were other people doing the same thing all over the West Coast. We thought he was the only one.

In 1947, phone lines were extended from Pete Pederson's house on Moorpark Road to Oscar's front yard at a cost of $154 plus the cost of telephone poles. The cost was divided between the four families on Olsen Road: Nick Olsen, Lawrence Pederson, Rich Pederson and Oscar Olsen. After the poles were set, the Oxnard Home Telephone Company charged a connection fee of $3.50. The phone set silent for days. Oscar and Tracy had little reason to change their habits and didn't know too many people who had a phone.

———————

Oscar's shop area consisted of a semi-circular dirt track dotted with outbuildings. The wood came from abandoned shacks of the original Norwegian Colony. The machine shop held the unmistakable odor of spilled diesel fuel on its powdery dirt floor. Electricity came to the farm with the Rural Electrification Act of 1936. The small building that had once housed the gasoline-powered generator was no longer needed, so it was converted to a playroom for his children. An electric pump pushed water from the well into the tank house and then into the house. Fifty feet to the west stood a honey room with a honey extractor. On my first visit to the small building, Oscar pulled down two small boxes containing labels for gluing his brand onto honey-filled Mason jars. He showed me a small stack of business cards with his name in sharp block letters. Nearby, a hen house and saddle shed made the yard resemble Main Street on a western movie set. Wooden and wire fences encircled a pasture where sheep and two aging horses grazed.

Every farm needed a horse; at least Tracy's father thought so. For a few years Silas Kelley held a side job buying up old horses to feed to the lions at Louie Goeble's burgeoning *Lion Farm*, in the yet-undeveloped area of Thousand Oaks. Oscar didn't trust horses because they were dangerous and unpredictable. Tracy didn't want a horse for her young daughters because she didn't have the time to supervise them with rattlesnakes and other hazards. One day Silas drove in with a pony in the back of his old truck. He claimed it had a few good years left and his young granddaughters needed it more than the lions did. Bowing to his fatherly wisdom, Tracy relented.

Her daughters rode the pony until they outgrew it. As teenagers, my mother and her sister acquired Loretta, a 16-hand mare in the same manner. By then the *Lion Farm* had become more sophisticated, offering a variety of wild animals and trained-animal shows to the public. Prior to being pink-slipped Loretta was a rising star, a circus horse *par excellence*. The mare's job was to enter the circus ring pulling a cartload of barking seals while the crowd shrieked and whistled. But Loretta was indifferent. She lacked a true performer's flare for applause. Even worse, she harbored a fatal flaw—a deathly fear of elephants. Each time one trumpeted during a performance Loretta bolted, toppling the seals. Louie Goeble finally got tired of the pandemonium and sold her to Oscar for fifty dollars.

Arthelia was the oldest daughter. She detested riding so Loretta became Jean's responsibility until she married and her younger sister Mary assumed ownership.

Oscar acquired Ben, a tall, raw-boned gelding, to ride while he poisoned ground squirrels on the Janss Ranch. When he didn't need the horse for work, his son Neil was free to ride. By the time grandchildren came along the horses were occasionally saddled for our enjoyment.

The farmyard held a small tack room constructed from the shacks of Norwegian immigrants who had settled the Colony a generation earlier. The boards were wide, old-growth redwood infused with the odor of oats and mice. A hasp on the door kept curious children away from the wooden boxes of varmint poison stored inside. Bridles hung on neat pegs. Saddles straddled homemade 2x4 saddle-trees alongside currycombs and liniment bottles. To my mind the presence of horse tack elevated my grandfather beyond the status of a mere sheep man. He wore chinos and a matching khaki shirt from J.C. Penney, and a sweat-stained brimmed city hat that kept the sun from his forehead, but the tack room with scent of horse sweat and leather branded our grandfather as a true Man of the West.

Tracy wore cotton housedresses, a one-piece undergarment and sensible shoes. She made her own soap in a dirt-floored washroom where she ran her clothes through a 1938 Maytag washing machine. The room smelled of lye and Borax. Among her supplies she kept an assortment of brushes for scrubbing stubborn stains and a small scissors to snip off oversized buttons before running shirts through the wringer. I helped on the day she used homemade soap for the last time. When she began grating off a chunk of gravy-colored soap for the washtub, muttering about her scraped knuckle and the unmelted glob that remained from her last load, I asked her why she didn't just buy a box of detergent from the store like my mother did. She looked at me with a quizzical expression and said she'd never thought of it. The next time I visited, the guest bed sheets held the scent of Tide.

The washroom had history. As newlyweds, Tracy and her sister-in-law, Babe, shared good times "making do." One of them owned an old wringer washing machine tub, the other a two-cylinder gasoline motor that sputtered and belched fumes. Oscar hooked the two together and built a washroom. Every Monday, Babe would bring her wash from her house near Wildwood Park in the back of her Model T. She and Tracy heated water, ran their laundry through the machine, hung them out on the clothesline and retired to the house to eat lunch while the trousers and work clothes dried on the limbs of a pepper tree that had grown gnarled and twisted with use.

After the last batch dried, Babe returned home to fix supper. On days when rain turned the adobe road into a quagmire, she hitched a mule to her old Model T and allowed it to tow her and her washload to Tracy's. She tied her mule in the gum tree grove until she was ready for the trip home again.

The farm seemed inescapably defined by its trees. The stand of blue gum eucalyptus at the bottom of the hill had been planted in 1888, by four Norwegians who needed a steady supply of same-sized logs for cooking and heating. The farmers sent away for the seedlings and their wives helped plant them in neat rows, in the lowland near the creek. The trees grew six feet a year into a forest 100 feet high, a ready landmark for the area. In the fierce Santa Ana winds, spindly trunks rubbed against each other, creating an unholy cacophony of shrieks and groans that kept visitors to the farm nervously glancing up. The undergrowth was littered with dried leaves and hard seedpods that five generations of children collected for necklaces to keep ticks and fleas out of the house and off dogs. In later years, Ellen Olsen strung chains and hung them in doorways for scent and ambiance.

Citrus and prunes were "cash cows" of the pre-war years. During the late '30s and '40s, Moorpark was the world center for apricot production until post-war reconstruction gave the advantage to Turkey. Local high school students vied for a spot each summer on Oscar's pitting crew, an excuse for them to camp out, build bonfires and talk into the night, meet other young people and earn money for school clothes. Tracy saw to it that the girls slept in the house, but the boys got to rough it in tents. It was the equivalent of summer camp and homecoming week, a huge social rendezvous that cousins recalled into their old age. Girls cut apricots in half and laid the two pieces cup-side up on wooden trays. Boys moved full trays into smudging sheds to be sulfured as a means of preserving their color and flavor. Boys picked fruit, carried the trays and spread the sulfured apricots to dry for two days in the sun. Afterward boys shoveled the dried fruit into burlap gunny sacks for sale to fruit brokers. Bags were piled on wagons and shipped out in boxcars from the Moorpark rail station.

In the era before refrigeration, dried apricots were a staple. They were candy, fruit and medicine all in one, a recommended cure for irregularity from a hard-scrabble diet of beans and bread, a preventative of scurvy, a source of vitamin A and C, and a treat to be carried in the pocket of every harvester crew in the Midwest.

Oscar maintained an apiary to pollinate his tree crops. At its height he owned 140 hives. In later years he became the Ventura County Bee Inspector, checking for "foulbrood," a disease that could wipe out entire hives.

From hill to creek the farm was steeped in permanence. Our great-grandfather Nils Olsen (pronounced Niles), had owned the land. He kept his name on the deed until 1940, the year before he died. Throughout his life he maintained that the land was everything and he safeguarded it with stubborn resistance to modern farming techniques and bank loans for as long as he was able.

We grandchildren enjoyed the luxury of sharing toys and playhouses that our grandfather had built for our mothers. We played in the same climbing tree and hayloft that they had. We picked oranges and apricots from the same trees as our mothers had when they were our age. We rode their girlhood horses and slept in their old bed. When my mother spoke of her childhood I was reminded that life did not change greatly from her childhood to mine.

Tracy's house seemed larger than its blueprints would indicate, but perhaps no house is large enough to store the memories that dwell within its walls. Although it is gone now, torn down in the name of progress, the memory of the house and the farm remains.

CHAPTER THREE

Lessons of Love

AFTER HER FUNERAL I found Tracy's photograph albums on a table. I opened one to pages of black and white photographs of a time I hadn't known. Her brothers in their younger years were a surprise: handsome, fun loving, with a look of ease that came from growing up without boundaries or restrictions. Her sisters stood before the camera; pretty, dressed in lovely serge and crepe, with thick coils of chestnut hair. In one, Tracy smiled from under the brim of a white hat, her expression one that I recognize in myself.

I found another side of my grandmother in the photographs that filled the book—Tracy in riding gear. I discovered that she had been an excellent horsewoman. Her daughters recall her riding even in her forties, on campouts and horse rides. Another misconception on my part— Oscar had been the one who mistrusted horses. I knew Tracy only as a grandmother dressed in floral housedresses. It was hard to think of her in boots and split skirt, an early Dale Evans.

A snapshot of her in a photo booth at Pacific Ocean Park with her brothers recalled for me the day that my brother and I visited the same amusement park, 40 years later.

Backgrounds of the photographs showed places and houses that I recognized, but in the 1920s, their porches and walls unpainted, the front yards sparse and bare. Gardens of the time were serious business, relegated to the back of the house. Flowerbeds and decorative fences came later when electricity, pumps and water hoses made landscaping practical and domestic appliances allowed time for creative expression.

Oscar and Tracy 1921

Wedding photographs taken in front of houses often included a chicken or two in the photo frame (free-range chickens and peacocks might offer an explanation for the sparse yards), or a row of tents pitched for guests to sleep in. Invitations to a wedding reception often requested that the guest bring spare silverware and coffee cups for the dinner. Washing, counting and dividing dishes and silver afterward was an essential part of many social events.

I was not alone in searching the photographs for memories of a bygone era. An elderly cousin recounted her memories of Tracy as we turned the pages of an album. The cousin had attended Timber School with both Tracy and Oscar. As she told it, Oscar stopped Tracy's brothers from pulling her pigtails. Years later, after they were both out of school, my grandparents met again at the Ventura County Fair. Tracy's father Silas gave Oscar permission to drive her home, and later to come courting.

Tracy's brothers liked Oscar. He was a plain-faced, serious Norwegian with a 200 acre farm. He owned a 1917 Samson tractor, the first in the Conejo, and 60 head of cattle. He was sober, industrious and strong as an ox, a staunch, God-fearing boy whose father was known and respected in the community. More importantly, Tracy's father liked Oscar better than her other callers.

Tracy had been courted by a wagon teamster, a feisty German ten years her senior named Frank Fritschle, but her father considered him too old for her. Silas met him coming in his wagon to call on her and told him to just turn around and not bother her. Their paths crossed again many years later, when Frank lived in San Miguel, California, and Tracy and Oscar lived ten miles away in Paso Robles. Someone arranged for Tracy's son Neil to meet Frank's niece Gisela, who had recently come from Germany to keep house for him. Neil ended up marrying Gisela and we called Mr. Fritschle 'Uncle,' just as she did. My mother cared for him in his later years until his death. It was from him that we heard the story of being run off by the father.

In her late teens, Tracy's new suitor, Oscar, bore the brunt of her Irish brothers' boyish pranks. Four brothers and a host of cousins seemed an uneven match against one Norwegian. Quiet and shy, and unused to children, Oscar made an easy target for their practical jokes. He would often call on her in a horse and buggy. Once, while he was inside the house talking with Tracy, her brothers hoisted the buggy onto the top of the barn. When he was ready to go home he discovered it tied off to a beam. Another time he drove to Tracy's in the open-top Overland automobile that he shared with his brother. Tracy's brothers rolled it into a dry creek bed. He had to return to the house and ask the father to hitch a mule to the front bumper to pull it from the gully. It was nearly midnight before he set off for home. He got only four hours of sleep before it was time to rise and start another day's work.

When he brought candy, Tracy's two little sisters rushed to grab the sack before he could knock on the door. For three straight Saturdays the same thing happened. He solved his dilemma by showing up the following week with two bags of candy, one for the little girls and one for Tracy.

The pranks weren't limited to Tracy's brothers. The first two times Oscar came calling he spent the evening in the living room visiting with Silas and his sons while Tracy finished the dishes. As soon as she hung the towel to dry, her father consulted his watch and announced, "Time for bed." After that, Oscar learned to help her do the dishes; at least they could visit while they worked.

After nine months of courting, Oscar stopped coming. For three months he stayed away—all summer. Tracy's family thought they had gone too far with their practical jokes. Tracy's mother made her husband ride over to the Norwegian Colony to find out whether Oscar had lost interest. Silas returned home with Oscar's promise that he would resume his courtship after the grain and beans were harvested.

Oscar and Theresa Kelley Olsen wedding party 1921

By the time I was aware of them as a couple, Tracy and Oscar were in their late fifties and had a pragmatic, comfortable marriage with the rough edges long since worn away. I had no way of judging the depth of their affection for each other. Beyond Oscar's occasional pat on Tracy's shoulder, they were not given to public displays. The photographs in the album provided a record of my grandparents' courtship, a love connection in the turning pages that grew with the passing years. Looking on, I knew the feeling of children watching their parents waltzing around the kitchen in the dark when they thought no one was looking.

The pictorial record included a photo that stunned with its honesty. It was of Tracy at 21, clad in her wedding dress, sitting back on a wooden trunk, laughing in absolute delight. She shone like a pixie, pretty, happy, happy. A granddaughter might wonder if Tracy, the most serious of her brothers and sisters, had chosen Oscar because he was the only one who offered; they seemed so serious and task-driven that they might have settled for a marriage of convenience. But in the photo, her face radiated anticipation and joy. Their commitment shows in another photograph of them standing on a porch, Tracy leaning into Oscar's shoulder, young, in love, expecting the best from their lives together. In the photos I found the answer to a lifetime question. Love is a family heritage.

In another photograph, Oscar stands staunch and rock solid alongside his Indian motorcycle. Hurrah, we come from adventurous stock.

Honeymoons end. The album showed the story, or maybe it posed questions that needed answers from those who were there. Maybe courtship is like eating dessert first; the substance comes later. A single frame in the photo album showed a stern woman standing beside my six-year-old mother and my nine-year-old aunt. Unhappiness filled her eyes. Despair convoluted her features. I asked my mother who she was, this woman with my great-grandmother's eyes. It was Tracy. One afternoon she provided an explanation. There had been another son, born in 1930, when my mother was five, a firstborn son who carried Grandpa's name, Ivan Oscar. In old world tradition he was to be the heir to Oscar's land and fortune. As a young Lutheran courting an Irish Catholic girl, Oscar confronted the inflexible power of the Holy Roman Church. He signed a paper stating that the children of the union would be raised Catholic. I can only guess that the condition galled him as he endured the murmurings of his Lutheran relatives. But through the birth of two daughters he remained steadfast in his promise not to interfere. When his son was born, he decided the baby would be baptized Lutheran in his family's tradition. Tracy found herself in the position of Catholic women throughout the ages, fearful that only Catholic babies go to Heaven. She pleaded for Oscar to relent and allow her to baptize the child, but he was adamant.

With ironic tragedy the baby was born healthy and died a few hours after birth, possibly from an Rh-negative blood issue. He was hastily baptized by a nun in St. John's Hospital and buried in a plain grave in the Santa Clara Cemetery, in a heartrending service that gave neither peace nor resolution to the grieving parents. My mother remembers her mother crying inconsolably, her father awkwardly patting his wife's shoulder, unable to vent the despair that lined his face. She said it was the saddest funeral she ever attended.

A few months later Oscar formed a cement headstone in his workshop and they returned to the cemetery to set it in place. But the ground had been disked over—the metal marker that designated the baby's grave, lost. They could not find the spot.

Years later the baby's sister Mary persisted in her efforts to find the location. She was told that the old Monsignor who had been in charge of burials kept few records, mostly in his head. But he was long dead and could be of no use in the search. Finally, when it became obvious that Mary wouldn't give up, the cemetery clerk admitted that, in the infant section of the cemetery, the babies' graves were still intact but the plots in the grassy lawn lacked markers. Somewhere in the jumble of paperwork, babies' names were noted first-name only. No way to know where the baby was buried.

Baby Oscar's cement headstone was never set in place. It remained in his father's workshop until Oscar Sr. died. Today it graces my mother's reflection garden.

Post-partum depression had not made its way into household jargon in 1930; a baby's death was something a woman was expected to get over. I don't know if Oscar ever understood the guilt Tracy bore over losing her baby twice, once to death and a second time in the quiet graveyard. It is not difficult to imagine her thoughts as she searched the worked field where her baby lay lost to her.

Three and six years later, babies Mary and Neil arrived, presumably when forgiveness was reached between their parents, the wounds of loss healed and joy returned. The house filled with family picnics and laughter. In Oscar and Tracy's retirement years, Tracy invited her priest to occasional barbecues and wedding dinners, but I don't think she relied on him to provide solutions to problems she could settle herself. She held a pragmatic reliance that everyone did the best they could, and let it go at that.

Whatever her feelings about the past may have been, Tracy lived and died a good Catholic. In the hospital room the day her grandsons and I gathered around with our mothers, it was the rosary that brought us together. We prayed over and over, "Hail Mary . . . pray for us sinners now and at the hour of our death. Hail Mary . . . pray for us sinners now and at the hour of our death." Behind Tracy's closed eyes, a tear slipped down her cheek and disappeared in the fold of her neck.

Some years earlier, in 1983, when my father passed away without warning, Tracy's heart nearly broke for my mother. She raged, "Why wasn't it me? I've been ready to go since Oscar died. Why wasn't it me?"

In his 70s, Oscar became close friends with his parish priest. During the last year of his life the two men passed many rainy afternoons in conversation about farming, travel and the nature of life. Oscar died in 1972. Tracy outlived him by 15 lonely years.

Tracy drove a De Soto, a dark blue sedan with leather seats and a tight chassis. Its motor purred above the sound of tires on the gravel driveway. If the car had a radio, it was not used. The automobile was intended for important occasions: a weekly trip to town or the occasional visit to relatives, never for spur-of-the-moment runs to the market for ice cream. The De Soto was housed in a detached shed behind the gum tree grove, a tiny garage of corrugated tin that had been built to house an early Buick. It provided a tight fit for the De Soto.

Before fetching the ignition key from her handbag, Tracy donned white gloves and tucked her skirts beneath her on the bench seat. Passengers did not eat in her automobile. To my knowledge no gum wrapper or paper scrap ever found its way into her car. Over 17 years later, when the car was retired with a cracked block, it was in nearly pristine condition.

Tracy drove with the caution of someone who learned to drive as an adult. She grasped the steering wheel with both hands, drove at 45 miles an hour and allowed little conversation while she concentrated on the road. At 14, she drove a Model T all over Los Angeles, acting as her mother's chauffeur. In her youth Tracy had been issued a lifetime driver's license, the same as everyone was in those days. A few years later she lost her handbag and had to reapply for a new one. By then the State of California had changed its policy and no longer issued lifetime licenses. Her new one stipulated that she had to reapply every few years like the rest of us.

She seemed to view driving as a necessity, not a pleasure. She never spoke of driving a tractor, and she didn't drive Oscar's pickup in her later years when they took road trips towing their small "canned ham" travel trailer. In her 70s, she relied on her grandchildren to drive her from her home in Paso Robles to Los Angeles and the Conejo Valley.

THE NORWEGIAN COLONY

CHAPTER FOUR

Land of Our Father's Pride

IN LATE JANUARY, 1886, five men and one woman made the trip from Norway to America in the steerage deck of a four-mast sailing ship. They were young people in their mid-twenties, friends and/or relatives either by blood or marriage, from the region of Stranda, along the Størfjørd. The journey to America included a boat from Stranda to Bergen, another to Hull, England, and by train across England to Liverpool. From there they took a White Star Line ship to Iceland and New York City. From New York City they rode the Union Pacific Railroad to Sacramento, California, a journey of 12 days. This was followed by train, ferry and stagecoach from Sacramento to Oakland and eventually to Santa Barbara.

They disembarked in Santa Barbara on a sunny day in early March, with the sun shining on Spanish tiled roofs and the tang of salt in the air. Ironically, the Union Pacific experienced deadly labor strikes in five states from March to May of 1886. They apparently suffered no ill effects from the mounting labor tensions because they made no note of it in their journals.

In the Norwegian custom of the day, their original names were determined by the farms they lived on: Uranes, Ansok, Overaa, Berge. After arriving, possibly at the time they signed documents to purchase farmland, their names were Americanized to Nils Uren Olsen, Ole Ansok Anderson, Jorgen Overaa Hansen, Ole Elias Overaa Nelson and Lars Berge Pederson.

The bachelors settled in Santa Barbara. Nils Olsen worked as a stonemason, reconstructing the walls of the Old Mission Santa Barbara during its renovation and expansion of a school on part of the grounds. Later, he set stonework along State Street that is still in place today. Lars Pederson, Jorgen Hansen and Ole Nelson found work as stable hands, caring for the horses, buggies and wagons of wealthy people. The five Norwegians gained a reputation for being diligent workers and eager learners. Frugal by nature, they refrained from strong spirits and saved everything they earned.

Lars and Karn Gjerde Pederson 1891

Two years later, in 1888, Lars returned to Norway for his fiancée, Karn Gjerde. She and Lars agreed that they would sail to America, taking the ship around Cape Horn, a longer voyage of many months, but it allowed her to bring her wedding gifts, including a set of wedding China dishes from Stranda in a prized wooden trunk. Two of Karn's friends, Lina Ness and Ellen Fjorstad decided it would be safer to travel under his protection, so they hurried their affairs and returned to California on a much longer journey around Cape Horn.

Their arrival was a boon to the lonely bachelors. The girls found jobs, attended services at the Lutheran Church and socialized within a growing Norwegian community that had arrived from the Stranda area beginning 20 years earlier. The girls learned some English, visited the Mission, participated in Spanish fiestas and enjoyed the coastal ambiance with new-made friends while they were courted by the bachelors.

Lars had lived on his own from the time he was 10, when his stepfather found employment for him and his sister with a neighboring farmer, following the death of his father and the remarriage of his mother. He attended church with Karn Gjerde and they were childhood sweethearts. He was familiar with horses and enjoyed training them to harness, a skill that earned him a position in Santa Barbara training carriage horses for wealthy Californians.

Karn was tiny, (4'11") and energetic, with a quick wit and a knack for baking. She had heard stories of the wild and wooly West and instructed her fiancée to go ahead and check things out. If it seemed safe he could return for her and she would marry him. The ship bringing them to New York also brought her sisters Suzanne and Lovise. When she arrived in 1889, Karn found a position with the Solanos, a wealthy family in need of a cook and nursegirl (nanny). She spent 16 months in their employ. They liked her so much that they paid for classes to help her learn English and later attended her wedding to Lars.

Ole Nelson

Elizabeth Berge Nelson

Some years earlier, in the winter of 1883, when Ole Nelson was 19, his father and two other men drowned in a fishing accident in the Norwegian Sea. His father wanted him to go along, but he refused, probably because the weather was bad. A storm come up and overturned the boat; their bodies were never found. Ole was the oldest. He and his three brothers helped their mother Martha make a living on the farm. One day a man arrived to tell them that his youngest brother while still a teenager had guaranteed a note for a friend and the friend had defaulted. Martha held an auction and sold all their belongings, dishes, furniture and even the family Bible. By dint of hard work and sacrifice they managed to save their land.

Ole was engaged to Anne Marie Ringstad, a girl in Stranda who would inherit her father's Nygaren farm. The father required that the couple pay her two younger sisters for their share of the farm, to insure they would have dowries. Ole immigrated to America with the intention of earning the money and marrying her, but Anne died of influenza before he could return. Later he courted Elizabeth Berge, Lars's sister.

Elizabeth and her siblings were born in a small house next to Stranda Church. Their father was a crofter which meant he farmed the church land on shares. A month after their father's sudden death, their mother was put off the church lands. The mother soon remarried, but there was no room in her husband's small farmhouse for all the 10 children. Elizabeth, 12 at the time, and Lars, 10, were sent to work at the Berge farm in the Stranda area. She eventually fell in love with the Berge son, and he with her, but since she had no dowry his parents refused them permission to marry. With nothing to hold her in Norway, Elizabeth accompanied her brother to America.

Elizabeth at first discouraged Ole's attentions because she was five years older and had already had her heart broken once. But he prevailed and they were the first of their friends to marry, shortly before the men obtained their land.

Ellen Fjorstad

Nils Olsen

Nils Petter Uren was born into a farm family on the narrow Uranes Farm, across the fjord from the Stranda church and accessible only by rowboat. The word Uren meant "rough place with plenty of rocks." They leased the farm but owned the goats that grazed on a rocky incline unsuitable for growing crops. A few generations earlier, part of the cliff behind the house had broken off, crushing the house and killing some of the inhabitants. Rocks and soil slid into the fjord and caused a tidal wave that washed the church off its foundations, spilling wood and debris down the fjord. Parishioners combed the rocks, rescuing what they could, including the baptismal font, and the church was rebuilt. The Uranes home was moved to a safer location against a rock outcropping on the edge of the property, leaving even less land for farming.

In addition to a small herd of goats, Nil's father Ole raised cherry trees, worked as a carpenter and fished. In summer the family climbed ropes to the flats above the farm and cut grass for winter forage for the goats. The fresh grass was tied into rope harnesses and lowered. It was stretched out to dry at the fjordline before it was loaded into the barn. The children collected branches and leaves in the same manner for drying. In the summers, children who had reached the age of five took the goats to the mountains to graze while they played with children from the surrounding area.

Nils was the fifth of seven children; his oldest brother would inherit the goats. Nils worked at odd jobs from an early age to supplement the family income, skills he learned from watching his father perform in carpentry and masonry. He served a year in the army and saved his mustering-out pay of $50, which added to his other savings, allowed him to emigrate when he was 26 years old. Shortly after he left for America, the family moved across the fjord closer to town.

Ellen Petrina Inversdatter Fjorstad was my great-grandmother. Her last name was derived from the Fjorstad Farm. (The Norwegian system of last names changed in the Names Act of 1923.) She was the youngest of three girls, reared by her father and stepmother after her mother died bearing her. Her family owned a traditional goat farm on a side-hill up the valley from the fjord that has been in the family since the 1500s, before official records were maintained. According to Norwegian law, her oldest sister would take over the farm upon her father's retirement and eventually inherit it.

Prompted by letters from other relatives in America and determined to make her own way, Ellen decided to immigrate to America with her friends.

Nils Uren's correspondence with another young lady from Stranda named Ingeborg ended unhappily when she chose not to emigrate and married a local farmer. When Ellen arrived in Santa Barbara, she was not eager to give up her town life for that of a farmer's wife. However, she consented to having Nils court her from his new home in the Conejo. She remained in Santa Barbara for nearly four years working as a housegirl until she married and moved to the Norwegian Colony.

Jorgen and Lina Ness Hansen (And daughter Ella)

Jorgen Hansen spoke English well enough that he was able to translate for some of the other immigrants. He obtained a position with a local doctor, caring for two beautiful horses which he groomed and exercised. In addition to driving the doctor around, he tended the flowers and kept up the premises as well as the pastures and stable.

He met Lina Ness when she arrived from Stranda. They had not known each other in Norway, according to her diary. Ironically, he and Ole Ansok made a pact that neither would have hard feelings if the other was to win her affections. Ole was working a ways away on the day that Jorgen stopped by in a buggy and offered to take her riding. She wasn't sure it was proper, but her friends were gone for the afternoon so she agreed. Jorgen must have made an impression because nothing more was written in her diary about Ole Ansok.

Her first position paid $12 a month, working for a family where the woman was ill with many children. In her diary, Lina mentioned that she slowly picked up English. When she responded at breakfast one day with a blush to something one of them said about her, they realized she could understand them and they were careful from there on out what they said in her presence. Jorgen helped her find a better position that paid $25, as a *nursegirl*, a house maid and nanny with the family that owned the wharf at the time. He helped her obtain a better rooming situation closer to her new job.

Lina was a shy, petite, God-fearing girl. The first time she saw Americans dancing in Santa Barbara, she had to remove herself. She wept on a rock and prayed over the depravity she had witnessed. Her diary described half-days off on Wednesdays and all day Sunday—with a requirement that she return by ten o'clock. Often her employer would be watching to see if she lingered at the gate with her bachelor. Jorgen's and her courtship was cautious and circumspect, with buggy rides, singings, evenings with mutual friends and walks on the beach.

Ole Overaa Anderson and friend

Little is known about Ole Overaa. He was unhappy with the land arrangements of the Norwegian Colony after he drew a parcel that he could not farm to advantage. He returned to his former job at a stable. Some of his relatives lived in Santa Barbara. He never farmed on the Conejo, although he continued to pay his share until the land was paid off. Eventually he sold his farm to one of his neighbors and returned to Norway.

───────

The men spent their spare time searching for suitable farm land, but each time they found something the price increased beyond their ability. This went on for two years. They would have preferred land near Santa

Barbara. The seaport town seemed familiar and was filled with kinfolk, but the land there was beyond their means.

In 1889, the Norwegians met George Edwards, an investor. He and his family were heirs to 20,000 acres of land from the original Rancho El Conejo in southeastern Ventura County. Edwards took them by buggy to see the property. He waited as the young men crumbled the soil between their fingers, walked the property and talked among themselves, agreeing that it was clearly a dry area of little rain and poor soil, but it was a start. He agreed to sell them a section.

Each man put his money into the kitty. The offer was accepted by the four Edwards heirs and a contract was drawn up. The terms were strict. Section 28 would be sold as a whole. If any of the men defaulted, his share would need to be assumed by the others. The repayment term was set at seven years.

Before the men moved to the Conejo in 1890, Ole Nelson and Elizabeth Berge agreed to marry. After construction of a cooking shack with a fireplace to hang her pots, she cooked for the bachelor farmers. She also maintained a garden and made their soft cheese and butter.

The land must have seemed like paradise to families used to ten months of snow—although, possibly not. Nils was moved to remark upon first seeing his new home, "There sure is a lot of rocks and sage brush here." But the land provided bluffs for hiking and it reminded them of Norway. They were well satisfied.

The land was divided into parcels of approximately equal value, using the appraised value of $4 for the flatland and $2 for the hills. Even though they would not legally own the land until the entire section was paid off, each wanted to improve his parcel as he saw fit. One of them took off his hat and placed it on the ground. Each man wrote his name on a scrap of paper and placed it inside. The rules were simple; they had discussed what would happen many times as they waited for this day. Each man would draw a lot, numbered according to the land map. They decided against each man making a random choice because they wanted no hard feeling between them. The outcome would be determined by luck of the draw.

Ole Anderson's name was drawn first for lot #1; 199 acres containing the Indian Cliffs and the bluffs, along with 40 acres of tillable flatland and the spring, the main source of water. Lars Pederson's name was drawn next for lot #2; 111 acres of prime bottomland. Ole Nelson's name was drawn; lot #3 for 97 acres. Jorgen Hansen's name was next; lot #4 for the 105-acre lot. By process of elimination Nils Olsen claimed lot

#5; the remaining 139 acres which included bluffs and a spring in addition to his flatland.

The men worked hard to make the division equitable. There was some grumbling by those who ended up with the rocky perimeters while others won the fertile "flats," but each received a portion of prime tilling land. Because he was upset with the rockiness of his plot, Ole Anderson returned to Santa Barbara and never farmed his acreage. In 1900, he sold his property to Jorgen and Lina Hansen and returned to Norway.

The men and Elizabeth worked long hours. The land had to be cleared of sagebrush and wagonloads of rocks picked off before the land could be plowed. Horses had to be broken to harness, hoes and other tools forged by hand. Shacks had to be erected, and boards hauled by wagon from the wharf at Hueneme, a two-day trip. Eventually each man could look across his land and see his neighbors plowing or pulverizing adobe clods with a horse-drawn plow or springtooth.

Little is known about the first years. Each used his savings to purchase his requirements, including a team of four draft horses and a wagon. Perhaps at first they shared farm implements until more could be forged. Some owned milk cows that supplied milk for cheeses and butter. They spared no money on luxuries; the men spent evenings at the fire hollowing drinking mugs from tree limbs. They forged nippers, plow blades and hand tools—even the nails they drove into their shacks—with a forge and hot fire in a common blacksmith shop. Hard labor made for democracy in the fields. The Norwegians remained friends and relied on each other for everything from camaraderie in their mother tongue to spare parts for harness and plow. On Sundays they gathered to read their Bibles, reread letters from home, share meals and picnics and take rides to greener parts of the Conejo.

They built simple wood shacks of roughly 12-inch wide redwood boards and narrow batten. Wood shingles formed the roofs. The insides were single thickness with no insulation beyond a length of cheesecloth or muslin tacked to the walls to catch the worst of the dust and sand. The shacks consisted of a bedroom and a living room/kitchen with additional bedrooms added as they were needed. Each had a fireplace built on the outside of the house with only the hearth accessible from the inside. It was here that they heated the house and cooked on black Dutch ovens hung from hooks. They did their washing in the yard, with men hauling the water and filling the tubs. They collected rocks from their own fields to use as the foundation for their houses and fireplaces. Sand was hauled from the Santa Rosa Creek where high waters deposited sand at a bend.

In 1891, at the end of the first harvest, Lars returned to Santa Barbara for his marriage to Karn Gjerde.

Jorgen and Lina Hansen married in the same year. They were able to rent a vacant house from her employer in which to hold their wedding. They borrowed cups and silverware, plates and chairs and set everything up. The photographer and minister arrived beforehand. When the ceremony was over, the bridal couple and a few friends returned the borrowed tables and chairs to where they had borrowed them, washed up the dirty dishes and returned everything. By the time they finished, Lina noted in her diary that Jorgen was suffering from nerves and exhaustion. He had to rest up a day or two before they could leave for their farm in the Conejo.

For the next few years when time allowed, Nils Olsen traveled to Santa Barbara with the intention of courting Ellen. He had been unsuccessful in his letter writing to Ingeborg and he took no chances. In spring of 1892, she agreed to come to the Conejo and stay with Karn and Lars Pederson who were expecting their first child. She and Nils were married at the end of April, when Reverend Leach of the Methodist Episcopal Church of Hueneme arrived to perform the service.

At the time of his marriage Nils built a small shack at what would later be the corner of Olsen Road and Moorpark Road.

Ellen Fjorstad brought with her from Norway a wooden trunk decorated with traditional rosemaling over cheerful sea blue paint. She placed her trunk against the wall of their new shack to store woolen clothing and heirlooms from the grit that filtered through the cracks in the wood. She also brought a wooden salt box that she hung from a nail, a utilitarian butter form and a wooden, chalice-shaped covered container for storing soft cheese. A pewter sugar holder sat on the table with spoons hanging from the top. Her walls were unpainted, with a picture frame or two holding images of loved ones or a favorite painting. Floral curtains brought a spot of color into the small, dark living room. Nils's pride and joy was a framed paper reproduction of a four-mast schooner that recalled for him his journey to America. Ellen's family sent along a goosedown comforter, and heavy knitted woolen socks and yarn as wedding gifts.

Ironically, the Norwegians did not see themselves as a colony. Others used the title to describe the five families with sandy-brown hair, green or blue eyes, who spoke among themselves in their native tongue and approached new situations with enthusiasm. The immigrants were eager to become Americans. Clearly they relished the opportunity to practice their English with their neighbors. Jorgen was more fluent in English and did early translating for the others, especially the women.

In the Norwegian Colony the spelling of names was apparently more important to the outside world than to themselves. The Norwegians knew their origins. If others needed to contact them, pretty close was good enough. Nil's father was named Ole. When Nils came to America, he became "Ole's son," or Olsen. Ellen Ivarsdatter Fjorstad was given the name "Iverson" by immigration officials. When Karn married Lars Berge, he had already changed his name to Pederson. Some usages later changed the spelling to "Peterson." Sometimes his name appears on official records as Lars Pederson Berge. Americans started calling Karn by the American spelling—*Karen*. She had no preference and went by both spellings. Lars's sister Elizabeth retained Berge until her marriage to Ole Nelson, whose name was formerly "Nilson." Jorgen Overaa became Jorgen Hansen, although his friends continued to call him Jorgen. Lina's diary refers to Lars Rietaa and Ole Elias when she writes of Lars Berge and Ole Ansok, probably because there were so many men with the same first name that among themselves they also used the middle name.

Normally the vowel 'e' denotes persons of Norwegian birth, and the letter 'o' denotes Swedish, but this convention was not uniformly applied by the immigration officials. In official records, Ludwick Olsen's name appears at various times as Ludvic, Ludvick, Ludvig, Ludwig. His family called him Lud. Oscar Ivan Olsen's name appears on various documents as either Oscar Ivan or Ivan Oscar. His father Nils's birth certificate shows his birth country as Sweden since Norway didn't receive its independence as a sovereign nation until 1905.

The Norwegians were as practical about their religion as they were about their names. In periods of good weather, a traveling preacher made his rounds through the Conejo and held service on the Colony. Reverend Leach was sometimes summoned from his church in Hueneme for special events and funerals. A traveling preacher made his way through the Conejo when the weather allowed. He preached in the Norwegian Colony among other stops. When any of the Norwegians traveled to Santa Barbara, they attended the Lutheran Church and noted in their diaries their pleasure at being able to do so. The rest of the time they gathered together to sing hymns and read from the Bible. Years later, Nil's funeral was held at the Methodist Church in Moorpark.

In 1896, Nils Olsen and his neighbors traveled to Ventura to take the oath and receive his American citizenship. The mandatory waiting period was two to five years. They may have waited to be sure that they could pay off their land. From that day forward, each new (male) citizen proudly voted in every election and discussed issues with other farmers. In many of the photographs that exist of those days someone is always waving a small American flag. The women did not receive their right to vote until 1920. Ellen was able to vote once before her death in 1923.

In 1898, eight years after they signed a contract with George Edwards, Section 28 was quitclaimed. Separate documents were written so that each man transferred land to each other for the consideration of a penny.

The Mediterranean climate and rainfall of the Conejo became sources of both satisfaction and puzzlement to the Norwegians. The women exalted in gardens and orchards where a seed grew with little effort. Each year they plowed straw and manure back into the soil, improving it. The men learned to predict weather patterns of their new home where each good year was followed by two or more years of drought. In years when the rain didn't come, the Norwegians fretted, mended tack, scratched seed into hard soil, hauled water and waited for the next season. They wrote letters to Norway about the abundant land and the ease of farming—and the number of rocks they had to pull from their fields. The journals of the early farmers recorded careful notations of the rainfall. Lina Hansen's diary mentions that one good year sustained them for the dry years that inevitably followed.

In December of 1900, the first storm of the season came with frightening force, bringing a cyclone at three o'clock in the morning. Jorgen and Lina Hansen were asleep in their shack on a rise with a good view of the Colony. They awakened to a roaring noise. It took a moment to realize that the roof had been sheared from the walls and carried into the field, several yards away. Wind plummeted what remained of the structure. Walls collapsed outward like playing cards, leaving the Hansens and their small daughter Ella inside. As she later recorded in her diary, Lina groped in the darkness for her shoes and threw a dirty rug over her nightshirt. She led the child toward a light flickering in the Pederson's window, where the three of them and a brother of hers who lived with them, fled to the Pederson house. Some of them ended up in the Pederson's bed, dry but in shock.

Lars Pederson ran to collect his neighbors and they returned carrying lanterns. Little rain fell, but massive wind prevailed. In darkness the men collected the family's food, clothing and bedding which they stored in the barn under cover from the storm. Most of the dishes had been smashed, but an unbroken crock contained cracked chicken and duck eggs, Daylight saw the neighbors sharing a breakfast of scrambled eggs before they separated for their own shacks and chores.

Within days the shack was rebuilt using the original walls, in a more protected spot in a willow patch near the blue gum grove. Ole Anderson had already sold his farm to Jorgen and Lina Hansen. They set their house at the edge of the new farm. Before the roof was reattached, Lina Hansen recorded that she spent a good amount of time scrubbing the men's muddy footprints off the walls and ceiling, but she praised God that the chickens and cows were safe. God had spared their lives and made everything good again. They were well satisfied.

Norwegian Colony (Olsen Road) looking west.

CHAPTER FIVE

Death Knell

EACH SEASON AFTER harvest, two men took double wagons pulled by a team of six or eight horses to Oxnard and Hueneme. They traveled by way of the Potrero/Long Grade south of modern-day Camarillo. To make it down the steep grade and over the dry creek bed, one man sat in the rear wagon, manning a hand brake. Often they lashed a tree limb through the rear wheels to lock the wagons while the horses skidded the load to the bottom of the hill.

In order to make the trip in two days the farmers woke in darkness, milked and fed, took breakfast and harnessed their teams before setting off. Leaving the Norwegian Colony at daybreak to arrive in Hueneme at about 2:00 in the afternoon, they unloaded, stayed overnight and departed for home the following morning. The sacks of beans, corn, barley and wheat were destined to be loaded onto sailing ships; the hay sold to liveries and horse ranches on the Oxnard Plain to feed the hundreds of horses and mules used for farming and transportation in an era before automobiles or tractors.

The route down the grade was tedious and required both skill and luck. One day, at a spot across the Calleguas Creek, just east of Camarillo near the Adolpho Camarillo home, Jorgen Hansen was gravely injured, his spine broken when a young wagon handler forgot to set the wagon brake. The wagons rolled into the back of the horses, panicking them so that they broke free of the harnesses and tipped the wagons. Jorgen saw what was happening and he jumped free, but he misjudged the direction and the load of corn fell onto him, trapping him. He was loaded onto the empty wagon and brought home so pale that his wife thought he was dead. The doctor arrived and set his body in a cast. He spent a year in bed in the body cast while his petite young wife handled his chores and his neighbors farmed his land. But he recovered and returned to farming.

In 1909, Nils' 14-year-old son Oscar was handling a double rig down the same grade. Their 28-year-old hired man, Martin Peterson, rode behind, holding the long handled wooden brake on the second wagon. They halted at the top to hook chains and a brake tree. At the bottom of the same Calleguas Creek crossing where Jorgen Hansen had been injured, they crossed a steep bank, forded the dry creek bed and climbed the other side. Something caught the brake lever that Martin was holding. He fell in front of a wagon wheel, unnoticed, and the wagon rolled over him.

Oscar saw that Martin was seriously hurt. He placed him in the wagon before traveling for help at the first house he came to, the Daly residence past Camarillo, where they normally watered their horses. The injured man was carried inside and attended to while Oscar rushed to Oxnard to unload the wagons. When he returned, Peterson was dead.

Martin Peterson was buried in the Olsen Family Cemetery. Oscar Olsen lost his best friend.

From 1893 to 1912, Nils and Ellen Olsen lost six daughters to a baffling illness that weakened their muscles and left them bedridden. The daughters suffered lingering ill health, each in turn showing signs of illness before beginning a slow decline. Sometimes the girls took several years to worsen and succumb. Some were born gravely afflicted and lived a shorter time. The oldest child was only a month old when she died. Others learned to walk and lived to 8 or ten.

Ellen Olsen tried every home remedy that she or her neighbors could think to apply. Doctors came from Oxnard on several occasions, but no one ever discovered the source of the illness. Some blamed the fact that Ellen fed her children condensed milk and the children didn't get enough vitamins. Some felt that anemia was the culprit. A web of shame wrapped the family for something they could not control. The non-English speaking Norwegians already seemed clannish and odd to their American neighbors. All over the valley, people gossiped about the probable causes of the children's deaths. Aunt Jenny, Ellen's relative, held the opinion that possibly Nil's soil was to blame. Nils's relatives held another view that criticized the children's mother.

Karn Pederson was the midwife who attended the children's births. As an old woman, she recalled to her daughter-in-law Vida, that she could tell when they were born, which children would later die because they were born with a stiff spine. Some couldn't walk, or took a long time to learn. Each of the girls became crippled and bedridden in the last year of their life. Three surviving boys remained healthy and lived to adulthood.

In their diaries the Norwegian women mentioned their feeling that God's will determined their lives and deaths. Their deeply held faiths allowed them to harbor no bitterness toward those who might have inadvertently brought disease into their community. But their hearts broke, especially Ellen's.

In 1911, Ned Olsen, 8, was standing in the yard when a run-away wagon driven by a hired man ran over him. He was crushed under the wheels and died immediately. His sister Thora, 7, passed the following year. Her cause of death is listed on her death certificate as tuberculin meningitis, possibly contracted from a hired man who lived with them.

Seven times, Nils Olsen made a small wooden coffin which Ellen lined with flannel, and together they said their prayers over a grave. When the weather allowed, someone rode for a preacher. Nils Olsen buried his seven children in a homemade *grave place* at the end of the road that later bore his name. For years, until the sun and rain deteriorated them, the markers were lined in neat rows:

<table>
<tr><td align="center">Paula, 1 month,
May 22, 1893 - Jul 17, 1893</td><td align="center">Nora, 5,
Aug 12, 1900 - Jul 21, 1905</td></tr>
<tr><td align="center">Nora, 6,
May 3, 1894 - Feb 4, 1900</td><td align="center">Laura, 7,
Sep 28, 1901 - Oct 17, 1908</td></tr>
<tr><td align="center">Emma, 7,
Dec 15, 1896 - Feb 21, 1903</td><td align="center">Ned, 8,
Jan 14, 1903 - Feb 14, 1911</td></tr>
</table>

Thora, 7
Jul 4, 1905 - Nov 8, 1912

Only Oscar, born between Nora and Emma, Peder Ludvik (Ludwick), born between Emma and the second Nora, and Nicolay (Nickolas or Nick), born last, survived.

In the following generation, my mother and her sister often rode their horse to the end of the lane in the late afternoons and climbed the little fence to sit among the graves of their aunts and uncle.

Years later, Oscar recalled his mother rocking the sick children, singing part of a Norwegian lullaby that he still remembered, "Last year, I herded the sheep in the hills. This year, I rock my baby in the cradle." He kept a small card hidden in his dresser on which he had glued the cutout figures of two little girls from a mail order catalog; life-like dolls with long blonde curls and bonnets, and a small donkey. As an adult he moved it to his desk where it stayed until he died. It was his grief card, the only image he had to remind him of his sisters.

Oscar's grief card made at age 10.

Ellen Olsen died in August, 1923, at age 60. In a quiet conversation she told Tracy that she was ready. Her daughters were all dead and she had nothing to live for. The coroner's report cited heart disease and a stroke, but perhaps her heart was merely broken. She was buried in Ivy Lawn Memorial Park, in Ventura.

In a cycle of hope and despair, additional births and deaths continued for the duration of the Colony. Jorgen and Lina Hansen lost two children. Lars and Karn Pederson had four healthy children. Ole and Elizabeth Nelson had two healthy children when they moved from the Colony. Nils and Ellen Olsen were left with three healthy sons.

In June, 1901, Jorgen Hansen and Lars Pederson traveled to Filmore to help Lars' brother-in-law, Ross Jacobson. It was the third year of drought and the land near the mountains had received more rain than the Conejo. Jorgen spent the weeks beforehand tending his wife and daughter who had taken ill with dysentery. Lina got it first, a serious case. She was quite sick when her daughter Ella was taken ill. With the help of Jorgen's nursing, wife and daughter recovered in time for him to leave to help out on the farm as he had promised. He was away from home when he became ill with fever, nausea, extreme intestinal soreness and dehydration. He was taken home and a doctor sent for, but he died within 10 days. He was 39.

Lina Hansen suffered nervous exhaustion from ten days of nursing her husband and the aftermath of his death. She was taken to Santa Barbara to recuperate. The neighbors tended her livestock and the farm until her nerves recovered and she returned. Another brother arrived to help out with the farm.

Later, the Jacobson baby came down with the same illness— dysentery, cholera, diphtheria or lead poisoning—the stories vary. The nearest doctor was in Ventura, a full day's buggy ride away. Others probably suffered as well, but recovered. Despite all attempts and remedies, the baby died.

Lars continued working, trying to help get the crops in. In late September, he fell ill with the same symptoms. He was taken to the hospital in Ventura, and assurances were given of his recovery, but despite all, he did not survive. He was 38 years old.

Again, speculation played its part. Some of the neighbors maintained that the men's deaths were the result of bad water, metals or alkali. Lina Hansen's diary suggested dysentery. When Karn Pederson traveled to Moorpark to pick up her husband's casket from the train, she found her sister, Suzanne Jacobson, on the same sad errand for her husband Ross. After the deaths, a dead squirrel was found in the well. The Norwegian Colony had been dealt a deathblow.

The Olsen Cemetery accumulated more gravestones:

Martin Peterson, 28. Died 1909
Jorgen Hansen, 39. Died 1901
Henry Hansen, infant son of Jorgen and Lina. Died 1899
Petra Hansen, infant daughter of Jorgen and Lina. Died 1895
Lars Pederson, 38. Died 1901
Ross Jacobson, 28. Died 1901
Clara Jacobson, 9 months. Died 1901.
George Ness, 31. Died of suspected suicide 1902.

With her own husband dead, Susie Jacobson had four young children and no means to provide for them. Her sister, Karn Peterson, invited her to move the family in with her. The two women and their eight children shared the shack for three years. Susie helped with the chickens, orchards and whatever needed doing. Eventually she married a man from Santa Barbara, Mr. Dykorn, and moved with her children to his home. They later returned to Norway.

Lina Hansen and her daughter Ella continued on their farm for two years, assisted by her brothers Albert and Jorgen Ness. In 1902, Jorgen Ness shot himself. Although the newspaper reported that it was the result of a gun cleaning incident, conjecture clouded the incident. He had recently returned from the Klondike, despondent and ill from his trips over the icy Chilkoot Trail, worn out from carrying heavy loads of supplies for other miners. He was recuperating in San Francisco when his sister sent word that he was needed and he heeded the call before he had recovered his strength. He was in his sister's small house, apparently cleaning his gun while the others were outside trying to round up Nils' herd of cows foraging in Lina Hansen's cornfield.

The neighbors suspected that he had let the cattle out to create a diversion then took his life, but they didn't say so aloud. The Coroner, Mr. Reilly, held an inquest and determined that the shooting was accidental, but the neighbors suspected suicide. Lina had also suffered the loss of her children: Petra in 1895, and Henry in 1899. Ella was her only surviving child. The Coroner's ruling of Accidental Death was a great relief to everyone. The combination of the deaths and the stress of the farm and probate tax problems caused Lina to suffer what she described in her diary as a "nervous fever." Her neighbors sent her to relatives in Santa Barbara to recuperate in the salt air away from the farm and its problems. She returned with plans to sell the farm, but with another brother's help, she struggled along for three more years as she sought to pay off the death taxes levied on her farm.

In 1904, Lina Hansen received a letter that her mother was ill. She sold both farms to Nils Olsen, her husband's farm for $3,300 and Anderson's farm for $1,500, which averaged $15.79 per acre. This brought Nils' holdings to 443 acres.

In 1903, during an exceptionally dry year, Elizabeth and Ole Nelson sold their parcel to the Pedersons and moved their family to Suisun, California. They missed the ocean breezes and some of their relatives lived there. The drought, following so closely after the death of their friend Jorgen Hansen and Elizabeth's brother, Lars, had broken their faith in the Conejo. In Suisun, Ole was able to build Elizabeth the beautiful two-story house that she longed for. A few years later they moved to Fairfield where they farmed until they retired. Ole died in 1945, six weeks after his wife Elizabeth.

In early 1905, Nils Olsen hired a carpenter, Martin Overaa, to build a larger house on the former Hansen farm, in the center of the colony so that Ellen could be nearer to her only remaining neighbor, Karn Pederson and her family. The home was a proper house with a living room, a proper kitchen with a wood stove and more bedrooms. It had a covered porch, bigger windows and a wash room. At the time they moved in, the Olsen's had six living children.

They had been in their new house for only a month when Karn Peterson announced that she was moving her children to Santa Barbara to be near better schooling and her Lutheran Church. She delayed her plans so that she could deliver Ellen Olsen's new baby, born on Independence Day, 1905.

Her departure was sorely felt by the Olsens, who were now the last of the original five families left on the Colony. They were grateful that two Norwegian sharecroppers, longtime friends, remained behind to farm the Pederson land. These two men helped Nils Olsen and his sons widen the Norwegian Grade in 1911.

The Norwegian Colony had been dealt a death knell. From the entrance to Olsen Road, the cemetery held what remained of a great dream. It was said that Jorgen Ness's tombstone never stood upright. Often when the Olsens visited the graveyard, his stone would be tipped onto its side. They would set it up-right again and dig it into the adobe soil, but the next time they visited it would be tilted again.

Nearly 70 years later, when the graveyard was unearthed, a little girl's coffin was found to be perfectly preserved, as solid as the day Nils finished it. Whether a matter of the casket set in a dry area or a miracle, no one was prepared to say. The cemetery served as an apt reminder of an era of Conejo history.

CHAPTER SIX

The Survivors

THE BRAZILIAN PEPPER trees that the early settlers planted must have seemed a strange substitute for the evergreens of Norway, but the trees flourished in drought years and in wet. Birds and wind spread the seeds. Today, pepper trees can be found along fence lines throughout the Conejo. Blue gum eucalyptus trees flourish as well, in small pockets at the bottom of the Norwegian Grade and as windbreaks on old ranch properties. A scant few remain at the original woodlot on Olsen Road.

The Butterfield Stage ran from the Stagecoach Inn, overland through the Norwegian Colony, cutting over the hill in a rocky crossing between the Hansen and Nelson properties. The narrow ledge was still visible in 1960s backyards at the edge of the Norwegian Colony, after bulldozers cleared the land to build houses. One side of the hill had been built up with rocks so that the stagecoach did not list toward the downward slope. The wash at the base of the hill was likewise filled in with rocks to provide a crossing. The trail zigzagged to Santa Rosa Valley and through the Tierra Rejada before the trail leveled off to Simi and Los Angeles.

The sight of the stage must have brought a smile for Norwegians working their fields. Some of them referred to the Butterfield Stage Road in their diaries. Oscar Olsen remembered waving at the stage driver once as a child. He found a spur and other items along the route.

In 1902, Nils and Ellen Olsen determined that Oscar should attend the Fremontville School in Moorpark. Oscar presented an enigma for the Moorpark School Board because he didn't speak English. But the Superintendant recognized a tax-paying farmer's right to have his son educated so Oscar was allowed to enroll with a proviso: He would attend for a year to learn the language, then begin first grade the following year. His parents would provide transportation or he would walk.

Oscar's parents felt he was too young to be entrusted with a horse, so the boy had no option but to walk the seven miles. The Pederson boys later attended as well, but they didn't walk with him. Possibly they rode their pony cart. Small and serious, Oscar was teased for his foreign ways. Some of the ranchers sent their sons in a buggy from Simi. He would wait until the buggy set off, then run and jump onto the back. If they noticed, the boys scratched at his hands until he dropped off into the dust. The following year his teacher moved to Simi and gave him a ride to the crossroads, cutting the walk by five miles until she married a man in Moorpark and no longer drove the route.

A wild portion of land with a barbwire fence divided the Tierra Rejada. On one side of the fence, two brown bears lived in a cave. On the other side Mr. Lapeyre ran longhorn cattle. Twice each day Oscar had to decide on which side of the fence he should walk. One morning he came over the ridge and found himself face-to-face with the bears. He took off for home and forgot about school.

Some days, Mrs. Lapeyre offered him a snack. When the days grew shorter, his teacher dismissed him at two o'clock so he could get home before dark. On days when he played along the way, his mother walked over two ridges to meet him. It wasn't until he was grown that he realized she was worried, He thought she simply liked the exercise. With her daughters crippled and dying at home, maybe she was happy to get out of the house. Or maybe Oscar carried her hopes for her children's futures. He recalled that she allowed him to climb onto the sink board to sneak bites of the Ghirardelli cooking chocolate she stored there.

One day, as an 8-year-old, he walked along the train tracks. He saw a man crouched near the ground with a long-barreled pistol, hiding alongside a train car. A mounted posse approached from Simi. "Go, get out of here, quick," the man scolded. Oscar slipped to a hidden place where he watched the man crouch under the train until he was spotted. The sheriff shackled the prisoner's wrists before mounting him on a horse for the ride back toward Los Angeles.

Oscar continued his long walk home with a story for his mother.

He attended Fremontville School in Moorpark with the Pederson boys for two years. During the summer a new school was built across town that added another mile to their walk. The children were required to cross the railroad tracks. Karn Peterson was afraid the trains would spook her sons' pony, so she made a decision to transfer her sons to Timber School in Newbury Park. Oscar's parents agreed that he should do the same. He attended Timber School through fifth grade. When the Petersons moved he returned to Fremontville in Moorpark.

On Oscar's first day at Timber School, four Kelley boys and their friend Donald Haigh were playing tag. They rounded the corner and one of them knocked their cute little sister to the ground. Oscar stopped to pick her up. He dusted off her pinafore and her long brown braids. She was 6 years old and in the first grade. He was 11 and in the fourth. Her name was Tracy Kelley.

———

In 1900, the Norwegians purchased a right-of-way for $40 for a road down the mountain that would provide access to the train and a safer route through Santa Rosa Valley to the wharf for their crops. Jorgen Hansen was in bed with a broken back. The County Supervisors offered to provide $60 worth of dynamite. The men were to provide the labor. The Norwegian men marked out the two-mile route down the mountain and drilled blasting holes. Ole Nelson set the dynamite and lit the fuses. They had managed to rough-out a narrow road before the deaths of Jorgen Hansen and Lars Pederson brought the project to a halt.

In the following years Nils Olsen and Ole Nelson found themselves struggling to maintain their own farms and those of the two widows. Because they were shorthanded, they relied on younger, less experienced boys to take the loads of grain and hay to market. The result was even more mishaps. None of the routes was safe, even for more experienced drovers. The Butterfield Stage Road was little more than a path through the hill, with rocks piled on the low sides in an attempt to level the low spots. Both the Borchard and Maulhardt ranches had double wagons overturn while trying to negotiate the early Conejo Grade—the second accident occurring days after the first, when the horses were spooked by the carnage that remained from the first. The Potrero Grade route claimed additional lives from wagons slipping their chains and rolling into the backs of the horses.

By 1904, only Nils Olsen, his young sons and two hired men were left. They worked sporadically on the grade and managed to complete a rough, one-lane road, but it was impossible for double-wagons to make the sharp bends. In 1909, Nils's boys were 14 and 10, old enough to help. The five, acting together, were able to widen it to two lanes so that two-men driving an eight-horse team could make the trip to Hueneme and back in a single day. They used a Fresno, a horse drawn grader, picks and shovels and whatever dynamite was available. The road took another two years to complete during breaks from their farming and schooling. It was completed in 1911. The Grade became the Norwegians' proudest contribution. Even at an 8% incline and no guardrails, it offered greater safety for man and beast. Still, oak limbs were jammed through the wheels to slow the laden wagons, especially at one extreme turn on the downhill side that claimed many vehicles through the years.

Ellen Olsen or her son Lud thought to take a photograph of the auspicious event, the making of the Norwegian Grade. Oscar is standing next to a hired man. His youngest brother, Nick, 4 or 5 years old at the time, is the barefoot water boy.

Widening the Norwegian Grade.
From Left: Hired man, Nils Olsen, Nick Olsen, Oscar Olsen, hired man.1911.

With the Norwegian Grade, Nils and Ellen Olsen were able to travel more easily to New Jerusalem (El Rio) twice monthly to trade eggs and butter for flour and other supplies. They could attend church in Moorpark. Later their sons could ship and receive items on the train. The hospital was a train ride away. Through the next years the roads improved. Eventually Moorpark Road was paved. When a bridge was later built over the Santa Clara River at Montalvo, the farmers attended the dedication with much enthusiasm. A pretty young girl was selected to drive the last stake in, to symbolize completion, while the entire county watched. After the speeches and applause, barbecued beef on a spit was served to everyone.

In 1912, Oscar was a teenager walking up the Norwegian Grade when he came around a bend and noticed a wagon stopped in the roadway. A big, redheaded man lay on the ground, apparently unconscious, with a convict holding a rock in his hands preparing to strike the fallen man. Oscar was farm-boy strong and quick thinking. He managed to disarm the convict and secure him. After the redheaded man struggled to his feet, he introduced himself as Robert Emmett Clark, the Sheriff of Ventura County. "Red Bob" Clark prided himself on not manacling his prisoners. In most cases prisoners honored the trust, but this one was of another mind. Although the story never made the newspaper, Oscar shared it with his children and neighbors on a few occasions.

In later years, Bob Clark's grandson, William, served as State Supreme Court Justice, President Ronald Reagan's Chief of Staff and National Security Advisor. Ironically, the spot where Oscar undoubtedly saved Sheriff Clark's life is within a few miles of the Ronald Reagan Library.

The Olsen and Pederson brothers seemed destined to live within sight of each other for most of their lives. The sacrifices of their father and the other immigrants bound them to the land. As a young man Oscar had just about taken the cure for farming. He would get up at five o'clock, feed and harness the draft horses, milk the cow, eat breakfast and be out in the field by daybreak. At the age of 17, he decided that his father was too harsh, so he decided to approach Mr. Lepeyre for a job that paid cash money and offered a more reasonable work day. In due course he was hired with room and board included. His job, as it turned out, was to get up at five o'clock, feed and harness the horses, milk the cow, eat breakfast and be out in the field by daybreak. But at Lepeyre's, he had an additional chore. Mrs. Lepeyre was sick and her husband decided that his new hired man should babysit the 4 and 5 year old children while he worked in the field.

Oscar didn't think a grown man should have to babysit, and he liked his mother's cooking better than Mrs. Lepeyre's French cooking, so after a week he quit and returned home. He didn't have the nerve to knock at the door, so he stood outside in the gathering dusk, wondering what to do. When his father passed by with the pail of milk he glanced over, saw his son and said, "Better hurry. It's almost dinnertime." Neither of them ever discussed the subject again. Oscar always thought that his father had set it up with the neighbor to have him work just as hard as he did at home, but he never could bring himself to ask.

Oscar was 19 when his education terminated with two years of high school. His first year was spent at the original high school in Moorpark, at the Fortnightly Clubhouse next door to his parents' new house on Charles Street. The school was formed when seven parents established a private, subscription high school for the fee of $10 per student for the ten month course. Mr. E.H. Holman, a former principal from Delano was hired as the only teacher. The school was discontinued after a year, when a new bond was approved. The new school would not be completed in time for Oscar.

The following year he boarded with a teacher and his family in Ventura and returned home by train on the weekends. In later years he took metals and woodworking classes at the new Moorpark High School night school. His 1906 Webster's Dictionary was dog-eared from the serious work of learning English as a second language. For his entire life he maintained a journal, noting weather and soil conditions, daily events and his own philosophical notes.

A favorite teacher encouraged him to become a train engineer. As a lad his father had shared a similar love of the sea. Nils had told stories of his voyage to America, the hum of the engines, the vastness of the sea and the lure of the unknown. During the three years he attended grammar school in Moorpark as a young boy, Oscar watched steam engines screeching to a halt, their bellies hissing as they took on water. Brakemen rushed to oil the brake drums while fireman filled the water tanks and shoveled coal into the furnace. He watched people disembarking, laughing and talking about their journey. His walks home were filled with day dreams of possibility. The train pointed his way out of the rocky soil and the jackrabbits of the Conejo.

In 1916, Oscar traveled to Los Angeles, as reported in the Moorpark Enterprise, "seeking to fit himself for engineering." He ultimately decided against taking an outside job and returned to his farm. His father had lost three fingers on his right hand, greasing the open gears of a windmill. Oscar was needed on the Colony farm.

By the time Nils moved his family to their new house in Moorpark, his older boys were in school. He was handicapped with his fingers, worn out from a lifetime of farming and needing an easier life for his ailing wife. Ellen had been diagnosed with a failing heart. Her youngest son, Nick, was seven.

Nick started second grade at Moorpark Elementary School after spending two years at Santa Rosa, the first to learn English. His mother worried that he would be deprived of a mother if she died. In September, she took him to the Ventura County Fair see the animals and enjoy an ice cream. Afterward, she clipped the announcement out for him to keep, after the *Enterprise* reported their outing. In November, she and her friend, Mrs. Hofflt, spent a few days at the Murietta Hot Springs. Three years later, in 1920, while the church and schools were closed down due to the Spanish flu epidemic, she cast her first vote for president. When Nils queried about her choice, Cox or Harding, she informed him that her vote was her affair. Senator Harding, the dark horse, won.

With school behind them, Oscar, 19, and Lud, 15, returned to farm on the Colony. They lived in the old family home. The two proved to be healthy, strong and stubborn. They formed an informal partnership, purchased the first Samson gas-powered tractor in the Conejo Valley and modified their farm equipment from horse-drawn to mechanical. The two brothers shared ownership of an Overland open car and an Indian motorcycle. Oscar took a course in tractor maintenance and shared his knowledge to keep the equipment running. When they both began courting wives at about the same time, they shared the car. Presumably, their dates overlapped because Oscar spoke of taking the buggy at times.

Oscar Olsen and his Indian motorcycle

CHAPTER SEVEN

Wives and Mothers

BEFORE TRACY AND Oscar married, Nils offered them the choice of the three farms. Oscar was the oldest son, and as such, got first choice, but while the couple was taking marriage classes and having their banns read at church, Lud surprised everyone by quickly marrying his girlfriend Hazel Mundel at the county courthouse. The couple moved into the home place. Oscar had no choice but to return to his father's house in Moorpark. Tracy chose the farm on the end, the plot that Ole Anderson had spurned for its grazing land and minimal flatland. The rocky cliffs were picturesque and the terrain reminded Tracy of Borchard Road. She picked a spot for her house behind the gum trees, on a rise where she could see her neighbors.

After her marriage, Tracy moved a few miles overland and settled in a brand new house that Oscar built for her on the west end of the Norwegian Colony, on a farm with a seasonal creek and craggy bluffs for grazing sheep. The house was a Pacific Ready-Cut Homes model purchased pre-cut for $2,500, shipping included. She and Oscar traveled to Los Angeles in 1921 to pick out the model they liked for its two bedrooms, cozy porch and built-in cabinets. When it arrived by train, Oscar and Lud drove two wagons to the depot in Moorpark and loaded the strapped bundles of wood for the trip back over the Norwegian Grade. Their father, Nils and some of the Pederson boys helped as well.

Oscar paid a Moorpark carpenter, Mr. Florey, $500 to help assemble the building. Each part had a number painted on it. The carpenter assembled the pieces like a huge jigsaw puzzle, working off three blueprints. The newlyweds lived with Oscar's parents for three weeks while construction continued. As soon as it was livable, they moved in and completed the interior details themselves, including glass cabinets and bric-a-brac shelves. The house gained attention as one of the finest houses in the area for its size, and Tracy's mother was delighted for her.

In later years Oscar enclosed the porch and added two bedrooms to accommodate a growing family.

Tracy spent her leisure time in her garden. Over the years she planted trees and roses, and flowers that attracted migrating butterflies. Her garden was virtually identical to those of her mother and aunts because her plants were starts and cuttings from their gardens, carried as gifts for their frequent weekday lunches and teas.

Tracy's ways must have seemed as strange to her Norwegian in-laws as her Irish father's had been to his German in-laws. Tracy liked Oscar's mother and was saddened when Ellen passed a year after her first granddaughter was born. Tracy visited Nils each Sunday after attending church in Moorpark. Nils was strict about the Sabbath and would spend the day reading his Bible and rereading letters from his brothers in Norway while his granddaughters played at his feet. Other times he would return to spend weeks or months at Oscar's house. Once, he admonished his six-year-old granddaughter Mary, when she sat outside on her porch crocheting; "You shouldn't be sewing on Sunday. Even birds don't make their nests on this day."

Nils Olsen and grandchildren. From left: Jean, Arthelia, Mary, Neil, Nils. 1936.

Nils Olsen with his grandchildren. From back: Jean, Arthelia, Neil, Nils (holding Jeanette), Gerry, Mary. 1939.

Karn Pederson sometimes invited Tracy to afternoon coffee with *krumkake* she served on dainty cake plates, part of a set that had been a wedding gift from Norway. Her house was always as immaculate as her manners and person. No one dared to call her anything but, "Mrs. Pederson," not even her peers. Tracy admitted that she never cared for Lud's wife Hazel, whom she'd known since they were girls. At any rate, Hazel moved away a few years later. For over a decade Tracy, Karn Pederson and Francis Pederson lived as neighbors on the Colony. When the Depression deepened, they gained a few more neighbors when Nick Olsen returned with his wife Sarah and their children. Lawrence Pederson returned with Vida and their daughter, Janet. By the mid-1930s, the Pederson boys and two of the Olsen boys were all back on the Colony.

In 1921, after Lina Hansen's daughter married in Norway, Lina returned to visit. Everything had changed. The prune-plum trees she and her husband had planted were dead, and that upset her. Her shack was gone. Another generation farmed the land with modern machinery that brought home the sacrifices her generation had made. She confessed to being adrift. While attending a Santa Barbara church, she met a missionary to China and decided to go there to do missionary work. She continued to write to her former neighbors, and missed the Conejo and the good times she'd had there for the rest of her life.

After a decade or so, Lina returned from China to Norway and is buried there. A photograph of the Hansens, a beautiful, hopeful family dressed in fine clothes, hangs in the Stagecoach Inn Museum.

———————

Nils and Ellen enjoyed their life in Moorpark. When he moved from the Colony he built a barn and kept milk cows for a small dairy enterprise. He brought cactus from the Conejo and planted them along his fence line for forage for his cattle—a trick he'd learned in the drought years—to feed the new spines as a way to save on hay. Ellen made her young son a vest to hold six milk bottles. He peddled around town on his bicycle, delivering milk before school. They never owned a car.

Ellen Olsen wore her hair in a loose bun. Her face was clear-eyed and kind, her nature task oriented and practical. She spoke with a strong accent. She favored a corset and long dark stockings, even after the styles changed and hems were shorter. Oscar remembers that he was eight years old before he ever saw his mother's ankles—perhaps at the ocean when she pulled her stockings off to wade in the surf. She lived her last years with a market nearby and her Methodist church in easy walking distance. She purchased a fancy velvet coat with a genuine fur collar to wear to her social events.

The Fortnightly Club stood next door. It was a ladies social club that met every Thursday. In 1910, its founder, Mrs. Robison, inspired members to purchase a lot for $75 and build a clubhouse for the edification of the community with the proviso that no dancing or alcohol could be undertaken on the premises. In later years the club collected recipes for their fundraising cookbook to which Ellen contributed Norwegian recipes. Women picked up donated yarn from the library to knit socks for soldiers during WWI. They wrapped bandages and participated in scrap drives. Ellen joined them, even as her heart slowly failed. She passed away in 1923, in her home with her family in attendance.

(Ellen Olsen's recipes From the Fortnightly Club Cookbook)

Clinger

Make a sponge like bread, in the morning put in 1 teaspoonful salt and a tablespoonful of sugar. Make dough thick enough to handle, take a small piece and work it with the hands into a long thin roll, form into a B shape and let them rise a short while, after they rise they are cooked in boiling water. Do not let them rise too much, test one by dropping it in the boiling water, take skimmer and loosen it from the bottom of the kettle, if it rises straight to the top they are light enough, but if they turn on the side they should rise a little longer. When they come to the top of the boiling water, take out and put them into a bread pan and bake until brown.

Fattigmenje

5 eggs, 1 cup sugar, 1 cup sweet milk; 1 teaspoonful baking powder; 1 teaspoonful brandy and pinch of salt; 3 tablespoonsful melted butter; flour enough to roll, cut in three corner pieces, and cook in lard like doughnuts.

Flatbread

Sifter of rye flour; sifter of graham flour; white flour; tablespoonful salt; sugar, water and milk enough to make dough hard enough to roll, roll thin and bake on top of stove, these should be rolled with a grooved rolling pin.

Nils and Ellen Christmas Dinner

Nils planted two orange trees in his front yard. In his old age, when little children stopped to visit with him, he would give them each an orange or two. It seemed that he was plagued with more than his share of hungry hobos. His teenage son, Lud, was poking around at the hobo camp one day and noticed a sign under the bridge, *For a good handout, go to Everett Street.* The men had stuck sticks in the ground near the fire pit with empty, washed cans hanging upside down ready for the next meal. The hobos of the era were traveling men willing to work for food. They looked like ordinary hired men, often in need of a haircut, their clothes rumpled, and always with a bedroll slung over their shoulder.

Lud had little heart for farming. He was social and loved mechanical things. In his teen years he enjoyed an occasional beer, but he was respectful about not drinking in front of his mother. Still, his mother worried that he might be lured off the farm. She lived to see both her two older sons married and meet her first grandchild. Fortunately she was able to do all three.

After her death, Lud and his wife Hazel wearied of rural life so he leased out his land to his brother and moved to Santa Barbara to work as a carpenter. Later he took a job as a heavy equipment operator on the San Marcos Pass and other projects. He rented a house on the beach and bought a motorcycle to enjoy his off-hours. Some years later, a small article in the Santa Barbara newspaper noted that Hazel was seeking a divorce on the grounds that Lud struck her with a 2x4 scantling (piece of wood), and that he kicked her shins and neglected to bathe. Hazel obtained her divorce in 1931. Lud's letters home gave another version blaming men, wine and song—a classic situation of people grown apart. The article noted that they had lived together for nine years, and that she asked for alimony.

He later married Irene McAfee, a gentle woman who had a son, Robert, from a previous marriage. He enjoyed his new role as a stepfather. Lud brought his new wife to visit the Norwegian Colony, and to introduce his stepson to his new cousins. The brothers traveled back and forth with their families to Santa Barbara many times. The three brothers and their father were together on the momentous day when Nils removed his name from the property deeds and transferred the land into his sons' names just a year before he died. He had maintained a stubborn hold on his land throughout his life because he feared that his sons would borrow against their land and lose it to a bank foreclosure. Nils maintained a fierce distrust of banks. His actions weren't unusual. The custom of the times was to wait until old age to transfer land to the next generation.

During the war, Lud worked in a factory in Southern California that made lightweight airplane parts from a secret DuPont product, "plastic." After the war he returned to work as a heavy equipment operator and bought a house in Santa Barbara. In 1947 he was diagnosed with stomach cancer.

When Nils Olsen died in December, 1941, he left property in Moorpark. In addition to his house on Charles Street, he owned a number of adjoining lots that he had purchased for ten dollars each or traded for a ton of hay. His holdings included a barn, corrals and outbuildings. His will left his two grandsons each a small rental house and his granddaughters each a vacant lot. His other properties were divided between his sons.

Neil Olsen was four when he inherited a small house next door to the Catholic Church. Oscar rented it out for him and deposited the three dollars rent into a savings account that he was not allowed to touch. Later, the rent was raised to $10 dollars. As a senior in high school, Neil helped his father put in a bathroom to replace the outhouse, and the rent was raised to $35 dollars. This was the mid-1950s.

My mother and aunt inherited adjoining lots on Everett Street, across from the hill where Nils kept his milk cows. Oscar tore down his old Moorpark High School and used the lumber to build two starter houses for his daughters. The lots were long and narrow, good for large gardens at the rear, but the County required that the houses be built with a shared driveway. Oscar finished the first house just before Jean got married. The common driveway was placed on her lot, reducing her yard and lawn area while the other house included a dining room. Perhaps this caused a bit of sisterly envy, but we cousins enjoyed living in a compound with each other for playmates.

———————

Nick Olsen was tall, good looking and a natural athlete. He enjoyed town living and intended to become a teacher. He and his future wife Sarah were high school sweethearts at Moorpark High School. They made a pact. He would attend Santa Barbara City College to become a high school woodworking teacher while she earned a degree at Knapp College of Nursing, associated with Cottage Hospital. They would marry when they graduated.

While a student Nick worked at a candy store that employed his sister-in-law, Hazel. He made the candies during the night after school and she rolled them in chocolate and applied the sprinkles and nuts the following day. Later he volunteered with Search and Rescue to find drowning victims in the St. Francis Dam disaster that killed 400 people in 1928.The Depression hit mid-way through his college career. Of the 200 students in the graduating class ahead of him, only three found jobs. He quit school, thinking the expense wouldn't justify the result. He and Sarah married and he struggled to support his growing family. Farming held no appeal; crop prices were falling below the cost of producing them. He leased his Conejo land out and struggled to find work. After several years of temporary jobs, including working as a furniture salesman for Sarah's uncle in Lynwood, Nick moved back to the Conejo and settled in the old home, renting it from Lud while his brother remained in Santa Barbara. His family was living there when Lud passed away in 1947.

A year later, Lud's widow, Irene McAfee Olsen, and her new husband Hank Haynes decided to return to the Conejo and raise chickens. Nick and his family were given time to build a new house on the portion of land they owned. They chose the saddle of a hill that overlooked the Colony, at the northeast corner of what would later become Moorpark and Olsen Roads. The cost of materials was prohibitive for a cash-strapped farmer. In addition to buying new boards, Nick used lumber from the old *Wuthering Heights* movie set that had been filmed on his property in 1938, ten years earlier. He managed to scrounge and barter for a variety of new and used materials, including hardwood flooring from the gymnasium of the old Pleasant Valley School in Camarillo. He sold lumber from his father's old barn to a restaurant in Thousand Oaks for cash. The house cost $7,000 and took the family two years to build. The day they completed it, the Conejo received its first recorded snowfall—a quarter of an inch.

Hank and Irene Hayes moved to the Norwegian Colony in 1949. They farmed for a few years before their deaths. Her son, Robert McAfee Jr. inherited his stepfather Lud's land on Olsen Road, after his mother's passing. In 1954, he tore down the original house and converted the chicken pens on his property into apartments that remain today, across from Cal Lutheran University.

Nick took a position with Camarillo State Hospital as head of the Furniture/Woodshop Department. He remained on the teaching staff until his retirement. Sarah accepted a position as a Psychiatric Nurse at the same hospital and was eventually promoted to Senior Psychiatric Supervisor. For the next years, between juggling his farming duties and job, Nick cultivated his passion for learning. He made 1/32 scale ships as a hobby, and created a 1/2 size stagecoach that he later donated to the Stagecoach Inn Museum, where it is on permanent display. He was active in Sons of Norway. He traveled to Norway five times to visit with his cousins, first with Sarah, who died in 1972, and later with his second wife, Jenni Pitello. Through his encouragement, several of his Norwegian cousins visited California.

Nick seemed sophisticated and urbane. He was Ellen and Nils's tenth and youngest child. He had no memory of his siblings or the struggles of the Norwegian Colony. As a result he viewed life with more confidence than his brothers. As the oldest, Oscar put his faith and energy into hard work and into his own family. Lud, the middle child, followed his passion for machinery and put forth a devil-may-care attitude. Nick seemed generally happy. He was a hard worker and devoted to his family. Both Oscar and Nick possessed intelligence and natural curiosity that created in them a hunger for lifelong learning. Life took unpredictable turns, but they shifted their courses and adapted.

Norwegian Colony looking east. Olsen Farm in foreground. Eucalyptus grove, Pedersons' citrus and grainfield in background.

CHAPTER EIGHT

Pederson Boys and their Mother

Peder and Francis Larsen 1924.

Pete (Peder)

TRACY AND OSCAR were already married and living on the opposite end of the Norwegian Colony when Pete Pederson married his wife Francis in 1924. Pete's land lay closer to Moorpark Road rather than Olsen Road, and contained an artesian well. Pete was hard working, more serious than his brothers, perhaps because he was the oldest and felt responsible. He and his brothers farmed their sister Anna's land both before and after her passing in 1955, from cancer. Each Sunday of his adult life he donned a neat suit, his hair neatly cut, and drove to their Lutheran Church in Van Nuys, and later Ascension Lutheran Church in Thousand Oaks.

With WW II approaching, the Pedersons heard rumors that the U.S. Army would be creating powdered eggs to feed soldiers on the battlefield. Egg production would be profitable. Each of the men built brooding houses on their properties and Pete set up a processing room. The brothers drove to Van Nuys to pick up huge boxes of White Leghorn chicks, trucked them back to the Conejo, and installed them under banks of heat lights. They began small, but eventually built to a scale of 15,000 chickens, with each brother owning 5,000. After the war ended, the brothers signed a contract with Camarillo State Hospital for 9,000 eggs a day. They took turns loading their crates onto one of their two trucks and making the deliveries.

Many of the remainder were sold to Howells Market in Oxnard, with a number available for customers at the processing room where workers buffed eggs with electric sanders fitted with fine sandpaper over a foam pad. Workers earned 50 cents a bucket. Afterwards, the eggs were weighed on a scale and loaded into a padded shoot that sent them down to workers who loaded them into the proper crates.

Francis Pederson died in 1964. Two years later, Pete married Rheta Lawlor. He lived another 12 years before passing in 1976, at 84 years. He is buried at Ivy Lawn Memorial Park, where his first wife Francis and his mother are buried. His father was also buried there after his remains were reinterred from the Olsen Family Cemetery.

Rich Pederson 1953

Richard

Richard was Lars and Karn Pederson's second child, only five when his father died in 1901. He was, by his niece Janet's telling, a man of great humor. He held a love of practical jokes, which made life challenging for his mother. In 1913, he and Pete completed their education, took their Confirmations in the Lutheran faith, and returned to the Conejo to learn to farm from the men who had been farming their land in their absence.

Two years later, Karn sold their Santa Barbara farm, which was located on the present day Hope Ranch. The sale of the land for $10,000 provided money to drill a well, and to purchase a kit house from Sears Roebuck, which she paid a carpenter to construct on Richard's land. With the new well, the brothers began planting their land to oranges and lemons, and later, walnuts, when a walnut processing plant was built in Oxnard. At one time they tried raising rabbits. They had over 1,000 head when the rabbits contracted a disease and many died. They had to destroy the rest and abandon the project.

Rich was Oscar's nearest neighbor and his best friend. They wrote letters to each other while Rich was overseas serving in WWI, and continued the practice as old men when they moved from the Colony. During the years they lived as neighbors, Rich would stop by to buy milk from Oscar every day except Sunday. The two men would talk over events and discuss farming while they sat on the back stoop until dark. They knew better than to traipse inside in their work clothes—besides, the men preferred the outdoors. And no dogs were allowed inside, ever. In Norwegian households the men might run the farm, but the house was the woman's domain, and she made the rules.

In the early years, Rich kept a set of four draft horses in his barn. He would harness them to implements before leading them to the field. Later, when they invested in gas-powered tracklayers and tractors, the brothers shared the costs of purchasing and maintaining the equipment used to farm their acres, going thirds on everything. At first they used horse-drawn equipment, but later they replaced them with two big Holt tractors and a three-wheel John Deere.

Rich hired men to help him with the work. One family came from Oklahoma with several children and lived in the hired mans house. As the children grew older the family got homesick and decided to return to the fertile valley where their kinfolk still lived. They hadn't been back in Oklahoma too long when they had a house fire. Rich received word that one of the children had perished. The Pedersons and both Olsen families sent them money.

Later, Mr. Ludlam came to work for him. The family had two sons, Allan and Richard Woolsey, who rode the school bus with Oscar's younger children and Nick's son, Gerry. Before the boys went to high school, the family returned to Odessa, Missouri, where they had come from. Their relatives, the Campbells, arrived and rented from Oscar for a year. Eventually they went to work for Joel McCrea and his wife, Frances Dee, and moved into a house below the Norwegian Grade that the McCreas' owned. The Campbell kids, Willy and Ramona, became Neil and Mary Olsen's best friends.

In 1917, Rich joined the U.S. Army and went to fight in France. He met a good friend named Pierson when the two served in the same unit. Rich took a bullet in his helmet during a battle that knocked him unconscious. Pierson saved his life, carrying him from the battlefield with bullets landing around them. They remained friends for life.

One day, during a lull in the battle, Rich played ball with a German soldier who was also awaiting orders. For a brief moment they were just fellows with a common love of sports. Neither spoke because they lacked a common language, but according to Rich it was the best moment of the war for him.

Although a total of 42 soldiers were drafted from the Moorpark area, none of them served in his unit. His family and friends back home were concerned that he might either be shot or, more likely, fall victim to the great Spanish influenza pandemic ravaging the soldiers in Europe and the world. His letters assured his friends and family that he was safe, but they were reading about a deadly, third wave of influenza expected in the winter of 1919. The influenza had been especially harsh in the Balken states, where it killed one in ten. It seemed to target young, healthy soldiers crowded shoulder-to-shoulder in freezing water trenches and exposed to the bitter winters. The influenza killed more men than the bullets did. The Armistice was signed that year, owing more to the influenza than to a military victory. Both sides agreed to cease hostilities before their entire armies were destroyed. Rich and Pierson were lucky. They both survived, but some of the soldiers serving from Moorpark did not. Rich returned from France in 1919 to continue his partnership with his brothers, farming barley and wheat.

Their expansion into citrus was enabled with the opening of the Sunkist packing house in Camarillo. In the 1930s and early 1940s, Sunkist trucks would arrive with a load of Mexican workers. The men would pick the fruit, laughing and singing from the ladders while their wives picked the lower branches. When it was time for lunch, they built fires in the rows between the trees and cooked their tortillas and beans. When WW II arrived, the border to Mexico was closed to foreign laborers. During the next four years, trucks brought German soldiers from internment camps in Filmore. The men worked in silence and the energy of the field disappeared. Rich made a point of warning Oscar to keep his daughters off their bicycles and the road each season until the oranges were picked.

Rich enjoyed playing tricks on his niece Janet. One day she dropped by to show her grandmother Karn her brand new car, but when she left the house later, the car was missing. She walked home in her high heels and explained the situation to her parents. They searched with lanterns in the citrus rows and finally found it parked down a long row near the pump where Rich had hidden it. Later, Rich sent her a wedding present —a neatly-wrapped box mailed from Camarillo. She opened it to find her grandmother's ancient suction vacuum cleaner, a relic even in those days.

Retaliation, no doubt, for the tobacco juice Janet would put in his orange juice when he wasn't looking.

In 1958, when he was 63, Rich surprised everyone with an announcement that he planned to marry Ruth Pierson, the widow of his best friend. Their marriage was held at the Lutheran Church in Laguna Hills. A year earlier he had donated 140 acres of his land to Cal Lutheran College, stipulating that an annuity of $16,000 annual income would go to him and Ruth for the duration of their lives. After their marriage the two retired to Santa Barbara. The chicken houses that sat on his property were repurposed into classrooms for the college.

Anna Pederson Albertson and Benjam Albertson wedding, 1914

Anna

Anna Kristine Pederson Albertson was Lars's and Karn's third child and only girl. She celebrated her fifth birthday just days before her father died. She grew into a lovely, cultured girl with wide, beautiful eyes and a stunning smile. With three brothers to dote on her, she was not thrilled when her mother insisted that she spend her school breaks in the ranch cookhouse preparing meals for the hired hands.

Anna met Benjam Albertson at a cultural event they attended in Santa Barbara while she was in high school and he in chiropractic school. They married in 1914, after he graduated from Palmer Chiropractic School. She moved across the country to his home in Minnesota, where he planned to set up his practice. They had two boys and a girl. Karn occasionally visited her daughter and grandchildren and the family sometimes returned in the summers to visit. In 1955, diagnosed with incurable cancer, Anna returned to the Conejo. Her children were grown and married and she wanted to be near her mother.

She and Benjam set up a trailer behind the main house and the two of them lived there until she passed the following year. Eventually, her husband remarried and built a house on her portion of the land, some of which is now included in California Lutheran University

Lawrence and Vida Landru Pederson, 1928.

Lawrence

Lawrence was one month old when his father died, and a young child when his mother moved the family to Santa Barbara. When he returned to the Conejo, he continued his education at Moorpark High School while farming on the weekends with his brothers. He graduated during WWI. He met his wife Vida at the San Fernando Valley Lutheran Church. She was born in Minnesota, but moved to Canada when she was three. Her father homesteaded in Saskatchewan with her older brother, while she remained behind with her mother and siblings until the house was ready. Her mother and she moved the family furniture in a settler's car on the train, a shipment that included the family cow. In Craik, Saskatchewan, they transferred their things to a hayrack and rode into the countryside with the cow tied behind.

Her parents died before the children were grown. She and her siblings each received $800 as their inheritance. She spent her money on a business course and worked in a bank in Canada for three years. Her neighbors, the Larkins, offered to take her to California while they visited family. She arranged a month's leave from work, thinking to return. But with her first glimpse of Santa Barbara, she sent for her things, took a job at another bank and stayed.

Lawrence and Vida spent their first eight years of marriage in Ventura, where he delivered gas for Standard Oil. They returned to the Conejo in 1936. Vida kept a meticulous house and was always perfectly groomed. She was optimistic and kind. They had one daughter, Janet (Reeling), who lived in Thousand Oaks and was very active in the Lutheran Church and community music programs before moving to Bishop.

When Lawrence was diagnosed with Parkinson's in his later years, he and Vida moved in with their daughter so she could help care for him. Eventually he passed and Vida married a long-time friend, Astor Thompson, a widower. He and Vida moved to Bishop to be with her daughter, Janet and husband Ken Reeling, a contractor. After Astor died Vida continued to live alone, until late in life. Eventually her daughter and son-in-law moved in with her in order to care for her while Ken built upscale homes for sale. Vida kept a sharp mind and body. At 95 she got her first computer and learned to use it. At 98 she learned bridge to keep her mind active, and still drove her car. She lived with her daughter until her death at 103 years.

Karn (Karen)

Karn Gjerde Pederson was widowed in her 30s, left with four young children to rear alone. She never remarried, and her legacy included strength, moral values and determination to honor her late husband, Lars, memory. Karn was a tiny woman, less than five feet tall, energetic and quick of movement and tongue. In the early years of the Colony her friends called her "Karn." She was a capable midwife and delivered many of the babies during her years on the Conejo.

She was meticulous about her hair, which she wore short. Her daughter-in-law, Vida, kept it home-permed so that it was always curly. It was blonde when she was younger, worn in a coronet of coiled braids in the style of Norwegian girls, but it turned a sandy grey in her later years. She favored an apron both in the kitchen and when she processed eggs. She was ladylike and soft-spoken with a sweet demeanor, but stern and determined when children attempted horseplay in her neat house. Her reputation as a baker of light, buttery cookies and cakes made her a legend in the Conejo. As a young, single mother she had helped support her children by baking cookies for sale to restaurants.

In her challenge to be both mother and father to three active sons and a pretty daughter, she learned to trust her instincts. She was living in Santa Barbara when a wealthy former miner asked to court her. He gave her a gold ring made from his diggings when he "hit it big." The ring had the words, YUKON written in gold letters across the side. In the center, a pick and shovel crisscrossed a gold bucket. Years later, when she gave the ring to her granddaughter, Janet, Karn explained that she didn't marry because she just didn't love the man enough. Her guiding task after the death of her husband, at 38, was to keep her children strong in their faith, and she succeeded.

She loved to fish. Often she would catch a ride to Ventura with one of her daughters-in-laws or her granddaughter Janet. She would bring her thermos of coffee, a sandwich, her fishing rod and an umbrella. She would request that they drop her off at the wharf so she could fish for two hours until they dropped by to take her home again. If she needed something from the store she allowed them to pick it up for her so as not to cut into her precious fishing time. A day well-spent was a day that she could bring home fresh-caught fish for supper.

In later years, Karn enjoyed her friends and neighbors when they dropped by to visit or buy eggs. Joel McCrea learned to wipe his boots before stooping his lanky frame under her kitchen doorframe. They would sit at the table while he helped himself to cookies from her cookie jar and a brimming glass of milk from her refrigerator. They would speak of the old days, the price of things and the world, she in her brisk Norwegian accent and sometimes quaint word choices. Even if she didn't attend Joel McCrea's movies, she enjoyed hearing about his experiences making them. Sometimes the Olsen girls would stop by to visit with an armful of lupines and an eye on the cookie jar where Karn's special crisp butter cookies were stored.

Each morning Karn took her seat in her son's processing room, clicked on an electric candling light and a small egg sander. She inspected each egg then held it up to the light to search for blood spots or impurities. If the egg contained dirt or manure, she would quickly sand away the offending spot and place the egg in a carton according to size. The neighborhood children were not permitted to ride their horses near the hen pens because horses scared the chickens. Any fright caused a spot of blood in the egg, ruining it for sale.

When someone interrupted her work she would click off the light and invite them into her kitchen for coffee. When her company left she would return to work. By the end of the day she would have processed her share of the 9,000 eggs before she returned to the house to prepare supper.

Karn arranged to have her Sears & Roebuck house constructed on her property before the family's return from Santa Barbara. After the other boys married and moved out, she shared it with her son Rich. She didn't drive so the family saw to her needs. If she couldn't catch a ride with her daughters-in-law, Vida or Frances. Rich drove her where she needed to go, most often fishing at the Ventura peir.

When Karn grew older, she began to have memory issues. Once, she loaded wood into her gas oven and tried to start a fire, thinking it was her old wood stove which she still used for brewing coffee on. As she aged, Rich hired three different women to help her, but eventually he moved her to the Lutheran Home in Van Nuys. He and his brothers would visit her on Sundays. She enjoyed her time there and was grateful for her friends and family.

Karn Pederson passed in 1960. One of her last conversations with her granddaughter was about a dream in which she was walking in the fields of blooming lupines on her beloved Conejo. She said that the first ten years of her marriage were the happiest of her life. She died in her sleep at 92 years. Her friend Joel McCrea continued to make movies for another 16 years.

Karn Pederson's Delicate Cake Recipe

1 cup butter, 2 cups sugar, 1 cup sweet milk, 3 cups flour, 5 eggs, whites only,

4 even teaspoons baking powder, flavor with lemon. No cooking time given.

Pederson family in the Norwegian Colony. From left: Rich, Pete, Karn, Lawrence.

Janet Pederson Reeling.
Karn Pederson's granddaughter.

CHAPTER NINE

Branching Out

FROM THE 1930s through the WW II years, Oscar and Tracy tried various endeavors to supplement Oscar's farm income on unproductive land with crop prices falling and production costs climbing. Apricots provided good return at a time when Moorpark was the Apricot Capitol of the World. Tracy raised rabbits and chickens. She planted a large garden, offering produce for sale. Often produce made its way home with Depression-strapped friends and relatives. Side jobs supplemented Oscar's farming. A job selling paint farm-to-farm provided samples for his farm when the cans were empty. A position as a custodian at the Santa Rosa School allowed him to give his daughters rides to school. He worked as a waiter for the Green Tree Inn when no one else would work for a Negro businessman. Afterward he built two small houses and rented them out, and later, used one to house a hired man. He poisoned squirrels on horseback for the Janss Ranch and shot squirrels with a .22 rifle from the window of his Chevy coupe. In 1949, he took a job as Rodent Control and Bee Inspector for Ventura County, where he worked until he retired. They leased their land out to a movie company. Tracy took in foster children whose fathers could pay for them to stay in a congenial country environment.

In 1923, Oscar and his neighbors built a barn to store winter hay and to shelter his sheep from coyotes at night. Eventually his flock increased to 600 head. Sheep could eat sparse grass while one cow required eight acres and hay in the winter. He utilized his rolling hills, bluffs and secluded pastures for forage for his flock.

In the early 1940s, he rented grazing rights in Chatsworth for his sheep and spent much of the summer camping with his four-year-old son Neil while they tended the flock. Tracy drove out on weekends and brought supplies. He hired a distant acquaintance, as a favor to Tracy's family, to serve as a sheepherder. Tom was a slight, malnourished out-of-work miner from Kentucky. A wife and teenage son came with him to the jobsite. They were diligent in their duties, but the woman didn't own a pair of shoes. One day the woman ran after some sheep and became stranded in a patch of puncture vine or goats head. Oscar had to haul her out of the field with a fireman's carry. He went to town and returned with a pair of used woman's shoes. The Kentuckian spent a day nursing his wife from a fever induced by the poison in her bloodstream. Later, the three of them managed the shearing.

Neil learned his trade at his father's side. Beginning the summer before he started high school, he and his cousin Gerry worked for the Pederson Brothers, baling hay. Their favorite job was driving the two horses that pushed the buck rake supplying sheathed hay to the stationary baler. It took six to eight men to run the baler. Labor was scarce. It was a time when even young boys could earn a day's wages.

Later, in high school, Neil sheared his neighbors' sheep, traveling from farm to farm with his hand shears. Once he took his older sister Mary with him to a job near Montecito. When they pulled up to the gate, the gatekeeper questioned whether this baby-faced kid in his crewcut, who could barely see over his steering wheel, was trying to pull a fast one. A call to the herd owner confirmed that Neil was, indeed, the shearer. The gatekeeper allowed him to enter.

At home, Oscar welded a rack to hold the long burlap sacks that held 250 pounds of wool for shipment on the train to woolen mills in Utah and Idaho. For years he would throw a ewe to its side and shear the pelt off it with a few quick strokes. When he finished, he rolled the pelt in a tight roll and tossed it to his son. As the sack filled, Neil would jump in the sack and tamp them down with his feet while he sheared another. The work was dusty, greasy and fraught with crawling ticks. It went on for hours or days in heat and dust until the last sheep was finished. When Neil was strong enough to shear, both of them would handle the shearing and someone else would tamp the wool.

Neil inherited an industrious nature and his father's common sense. Whenever a sunny day led him to gaze out the window of his classroom, the teacher would send him out to hoe weeds with the janitor. She told him on several occasions that he was only going to be a farmer and he didn't need as much education as a town boy. Ironically, he later graduated from college and handled the land development of his ranch, using skills the teacher probably didn't anticipate him needing.

When he was 10, Neil began rebuilding the engine on his father's worn-out Studebaker. It took him two years. While he was fixing it up, he drove it using a wooden block so he could see over the steering wheel to drive down the grade. Later he had an old green sedan that he drove to school. When someone pointed out that it was green, not tan, he realized he was color blind.

———————

Our grandparents taught us a philosophy of life without saying a word. They valued hard work, common sense and logic above all else. Oscar would have snorted at the idea of a drowning warning label on a plastic bucket. He showed us how to don a beekeeper's veil and walk among his buzzing hives. He rarely emerged with a red welt; the bees knew him and allowed him to share their world. "Use your head," he used to say. "That's what it's there for." For him and his brother Nick, the safety of their children and grandchildren depended on learning where danger lurked. Their children spent their days walking the rattlesnake infested hills of the Conejo, exploring the world of nature. They learned to avoid the flywheels of tractors, irrigation ponds, rattlesnakes and overhead power lines, to anticipate the unexpected, to use caution around a horse and stay out of the nests when the owls were sitting. Abstract ideas were fine, but farm kids were doers. Farmers learned to invent, reinvent and improvise in a cash-poor economy. Like most men of their generation, they prided themselves on self-sufficiency and shared their skills with anyone who asked.

The Olsens and Pedersons of the Norwegian Colony were methodical, innovative and thrifty. The Pedersons saved their money and shared everything they could. They repaired their tractors and sometimes held them together with bailing wire. Oscar and Rich kept bees to pollinate their citrus and apricot trees. Oscar sold honey under his own label. He and Nick tore down their former school in Moorpark, as well as their father's old barn to build houses. In the evenings when work was finished, they used their lathes to turn apricot limbs into candlesticks and bowls, just as their father had done before them. Nick became a master craftsman, largely self-taught.

After he retired, Oscar built cherrywood jewelry boxes for each of his daughters and granddaughters, and bureaus and hutches to hold their dishes. He taught his grandchildren to collect stamps, coins and rocks, with trips into the deserts to gather them. Later, he polished and set the stones. His mail contained subscription magazines that included many diverse interests, including travel, gardening, bee keeping, politics, art and world events. He and Tracy read every page and passed them on to us.

They instilled in their grandchildren a lifelong love of learning. Their gifts to me were books: *Olaf and Anne, Children of Norway; The Great Journey of Marquette and Joliette*. Monthly subscriptions to *Calling All Girls* and *Boy's Life*. For high school graduation, *The Anthology of World Literature in Digest Form*. They seemed to understand their grandchildren's needs better than we did at the time.

Throughout her life Tracy controlled her own inheritance, 175 acres of prime Conejo farmland. She kept the land in her name and handled her own finances. Grandchildren grew up understanding that men and women could have separate checking accounts, that sisters discussed taxes and real estate as well as hollyhocks and babies when they got together for afternoon tea. Tracy was respected as much for her independent means as for her position as mother and grandmother. In the years before Women's Lib, her granddaughters watched and learned how things could be done.

Tracy's discipline began early. After graduating from grammar school in 1914, she was able to attend high school in Oxnard for two years, commuting from the Conejo. Her brothers drove her to Oxnard to stay with relatives and returned for her on Friday afternoons so she could help her mother with weekend chores. Her report card for the year of 1915-16 showed no days absent, no days tardy and straight 1's, the equivalent of A's.

In retirement, Oscar established traditions that seemed to fill a yearning from his youth. Each Christmas he handed out boxes of chocolate covered cherries he purchased from Sprouse-Reitz by the case. It didn't matter whether we loved the candy or not, it was the thought that counted.

He was a curious, observant traveler in his later years. His photography instruments ranged from a simple Brownie camera to one of the first Polaroid cameras on the market. Eventually he replaced it with a slide camera, and a projector and screen for the hundreds of slides from each trip they took. His hour-long slide shows of national parks and public gardens caused younger children to fall asleep on the carpet and teens' eyes to glaze over, but we understood his love of photography, travel and discovery—and his desire to expose us to the larger world. Crowded together on footstools and sofas, a family celebrated its roots (and wondered why Oscar seldom included a single person in his photos). Curiously, the years when life was lived at a slower pace seemed to create more lasting memories.

Uncle Nick taught us that farm children could aspire to college and travel to distant lands, learn a foreign language and return with new friends and stories. Nick complemented Oscar's experiences. As a young adult, seeing weathered, white-haired brothers hunkered over a meal at the kitchen table created an understanding of family and future in me that has endured.

Nils and Ellen Olsen with sons Nick, Oscar and Lud, 1920.

BORCHARD

CHAPTER TEN

German Pragmatists

CASPAR BORCHARD SR. was born in Werxhausen, Germany in 1842. As a young man he traveled from a small town in Germany to buy a farm in America. Once established, he returned home to find a wife. At the Stagecoach Inn Museum, a docent told our group that when Caspar's first wife died, he returned to his hometown in Germany, stood on a tavern table and announced, "I'm rich, I'm from America. I'm looking for a wife. Do I have any takers?" According to the docent, someone mentioned the offer to a relative, Theresa Maring, and an arrangement was struck.

In point of fact, Caspar Borchard Sr.'s path to the Conejo was a bit more circuitous and a lot less swashbuckling. His uncle Christian had departed from Hanover, Germany, for California two years earlier and failed to send word of his whereabouts home to his anxious mother. His well-to-do family worried. They had a secondary reason for pressing Caspar to go in search of his relative. Caspar, 22, faced conscription into the German army. A trip to California was the safer choice.

Eventually, he found his uncle in Antioch, farming. After working for a time in Antioch, Caspar bought 1,000 acres near Oxnard, but had some difficulty transferring the funds to pay for it. He decided he must return to Germany to attend to the details. While waiting to board the ship he was invited by a stranger to have a drink. Not accustomed to strong spirits, he found his new friend pressing one drink after another on him as he tried unsuccessfully to decline. Upon leaving the bar he tripped or was struck, and awoke to find his money missing from his waistcoat. With his passage money gone he had no choice but to let the boat sail without him. Penniless and despairing, he was forced to forfeit the land-purchase and to return to Antioch to work for new passage money home.

A few years later, after farming in Ventura County, he sailed again for Germany and returned to America with money to rent land in Ventura County. The venture went well. A few more years passed until he was secure enough that he could consider returning to Germany again, this time to arrange funds to buy his farm and perhaps to find a suitable wife. He arranged for his brother to farm the land until he could return to purchase it. With his future secured, he sailed to Germany in 1871. In November, he married Theresa Diedrich, a delicate, pretty girl from his home town of Werxhausen. They were due to return to California, but her parents prevailed upon him to put off the trip until their daughter's health improved. He agreed, unwilling to see his in-laws suffer. He expected to leave again within a few months, but instead of improving, his bride's health declined. They remained in Germany until she passed, three years later.

Caspar buried his wife and waited through the customary mourning year. When the year was up, he married Theresa Maring, the daughter of a neighbor. The day following his marriage, September 29, 1875, the two sailed for California with money to purchase his land.

Caspar found his brother John and wife comfortably settled on his rented farm. They had expected to care-take for less than a year, but it had been nearly five. Caspar could scarcely expect them to leave. Instead, he bought 200 acres of bottomland from Godfrey Maulhardt. He farmed it for nine years while keeping an eye out for a larger farm to support his growing family. Eventually his need for larger acreage sent him to the Conejo Valley.

The valley had been home to Chumash Indians who gathered acorns from a thousand oaks, their principle source of food. They left their gentle mark on the land until Jose de la Guerra petitioned the Spanish King for a deed, after a former grantee abandoned interest in the valley. In its rural heyday, thousands of acres lay in a flat valley surrounded by whale-humped knolls covered with native grasses that had never felt the cut of till or furrow. During 1860, William H. Brewer passed through the valley on his way from the San Fernando Valley to Buenaventura, on his first geological survey through California. He had been commissioned to crisscross the terrain, map his findings and report back to the legislature exactly what the new state contained in terms of resources and size. He reported that the valley was bordered on all sides by rugged mountains and exited by a steep grade that tested the skills of his teamster, Jack.

Brewer's path took him through the Rancho Trifuno; within a few days he passed on to explore other vistas. His journey through the "beautiful valley" was distilled to little more than a paragraph in his journal.

In 1888, Caspar Sr., Theresa and their children moved to the Conejo. They obtained some of their new farm from the bank in a forced sale when James Hammell, owner of the Grand Union Hotel in Newbury Park lost it in a drought year. The rest of the ranch was purchased piecemeal: 3,115 acres from one man and 1,047 acres from another. Caspar Sr. paid them a total of $6,366, according to two deeds of sale. The cost averaged to $6.08 per acre. The land must have been a bargain for a farmer like Caspar Sr. with a number of healthy young sons to help farm.

The Ventura County Star Free Press reported on May 5, 1893, that Caspar Borchard Sr. had built one of the largest barns in the county. It stood on the Conejo and measured 72 feet by 100 feet by 36 ½ feet in height. By this date his family had expanded to include: Rosa, 17, Mary, 15, Leo, 14, Caspar Jr., 12, Antone, 10, Frank, 8, Charles, 5, and Teresa, 3.

Thirty-two horse harvest team on the Conejo.

Antone Borchard pumping water on the Conejo

As the boys grew older they used their unproductive land for grazing. At one time, 1,700 head of goats and sheep foraged the hillsides. With his sons' help the father built outbuildings for a slaughtering and meat-cutting business. They planted pasture for their herd of high-grade mules and over 100 horses, including Norman-Percheron draft horses bred from stallions brought on board ship from Germany. Farmers came from far distances to purchase them for pulling their threshing machines.

The flatland yielded its promise in wet years and in dry. An experimental farmer, Borchard, and later his sons and son-in-law, introduced crops that were new to the area, including tomatoes, giant pumpkins, walnuts, grain. They made charcoal from the smaller oaks and planted apricot trees on some of the cleared land.

In late summer the boys operated a huge threshing machine, possibly in conjunction with a neighbor named Waddey. It was pulled by a team of horses in five rows of six abreast, with two of the most trusted as guides. On smaller fields ripe barley or wheat was raked into windrows and fed to the stationary thresher with big buck rakes. On threshing day, men with pitchforks loaded it to feed the thresher. The threshed grain was poured into gunny sacks, the openings stitched shut, bags hefted onto flatbed wagons and hauled to the Hueneme Wharf for sale in Europe. Nothing was wasted. The straw was sold as bedding for horse stables and gardens—and even as mattress filler.

The thresher was moved around to neighboring farms. Antone Borchard handled the jerk lines, gradually increasing the number of horses under his control until he handled a team of 32 draft horses. His team pulled a huge Holt harvester and thresher used to reap the golden grain of Ventura County. Controlling the horses was a muscle-wrenching activity that taxed a man's physical strength and required a deep understanding of equine psychology.

When fall brought the end of the harvest season, the residents of the Conejo came together to dance and make merry, most often in Caspar Sr.'s barn after the grain crop was taken to market. Local musicians took turns playing while farmers and their wives danced and enjoyed potluck dinner with their babies asleep on blankets in the corner.

The early history of the Conejo was marked with stories of boom and bust, drought and disease besting the efforts of struggling farmers and stockman. Farms changed hands as owners sold out, went broke or moved on. The Grand Hotel failed when the stagecoach route bypassed it and was diverted to the Santa Rosa Valley. Later, the railroad chose to connect Ventura to the Los Angeles basin with a track that passed through Moorpark and the Simi Valley without a barrier of mountains or a steep grade.

Caspar Sr.'s methodical practices allowed him to add to the family holdings. At one time he owned 10,000 acres in Ventura County, perhaps an equal amount in Orange County, and two ranches in Texas that totaled 8,000 acres.

Theresa bore eight children: three girls; Rosa, Mary and Teresa and five boys; Leo, Caspar Jr., Antone, Frank and Charles. Her older daughters were in their early 20s when she died at 49, of stomach cancer. Her death came unexpectedly. She was feeling poorly so her husband rushed her to a doctor's office in Ventura. The doctor examined her and determined that she needed to be hospitalized. After a day's rest at a relative's house in Ventura, she was reloaded into the back of Caspar's spring wagon, on a mattress he had placed there for her comfort. When daylight arrived he headed the buggy toward St. Vincent Hospital in Los Angeles. The cancer was too advanced. She was taken home to die.

Her children recall that her last request, as they pressed against her deathbed, was that they "go to church all of your lives." To a one, they complied.

After her mother's death, Mary, the second and most practical of the girls, assumed the job of caring for her father and raising her younger brothers and sisters. In the family it was told that Mary turned down an offer of marriage to devote her life to her siblings. After her sisters married and had families of their own, Mary continued to keep house for her father. Following his death she had a small house built behind her sister's in order to assist Teresa with much of the cooking, cleaning and care of the children. She leased her inherited land to her brother-in-law to farm.

When her nieces grew to adulthood she visited their houses, bringing flowers and vegetables from her garden. Their Wednesday visits gave the hardworking women something to look forward to. The visits also provided an opportunity for the ladies to exchange family news. My grandmother, Tracy, was much older than her sisters. Her mother, Rosa, married several years before her sister, so our line held the oldest daughter of the oldest daughter for several generations. I was allowed to serve tea and cakes to the ladies when they met at our house. I listened to stories and watched the way that sisters interacted. It was heady information for a girl of ten.

Mary Borchard seemed stern and sensible. Her sister Rosa, my great-grandmother, seemed quieter and gentle. They were each tall, thin and hale from a lifetime of hard work. In 1924, they joined a group of 14 other cousins for a trip to the East Coast and Europe to visit relatives in Germany and to see the homeland.

Rosa spoke in a thin voice and wore her hair in a coil for everyday— probably twisted quickly into place before daybreak brought the first chores. Her husband Silas was a sociable, well-liked Irishman who spun the best yarns in the valley and liked to supervise when there was a job to be done. Rosa met him when he came to work for her father on the Borchard Ranch. They married in 1899, when she was twenty-three.

Rosa and her sister Mary were born in New Jerusalem, the original name for El Rio, on the east end of Oxnard. Later, they attended Ocean View School in Hueneme. The younger children attended Timber District School when classes were held in the Stagecoach Inn—and parochial school in Los Angeles while living with an aunt. She was able to visit Germany. Her sister Teresa was much younger. Their widowed father arranged for Theresa to attend school and live with their relatives in Hanover, Germany.

Caspar Sr. retired in 1918, at the age of 76 years. He gifted each of his children with $12,000 and 1,000 acres. He took them to the top of the Conejo Grade and pointed out how he planned to divide the land using creeks, roads and natural boundaries. Four of the boys, Frank, Antone, Charles and Leo, chose to make their homes on holdings in Orange County. Rosa, Teresa, Mary and Caspar Jr. remained in the Conejo.

In 1928, the family gathered in San Fernando to celebrate Caspar Sr.'s 86th birthday at a barbecue attended by 130 relatives and friends.

Caspar Borchard Sr. with sons and sons-in-law on his 86th birthday, 1928.

Caspar Borchard Sr. with his daughters and daughters-in-law in 1928.

Through the years each of the brothers managed to increase their holdings. Antone drained swampland in Santa Ana and acquired nearly 1,000 acres of prime farmland, doubling his holding. He and his brothers were pioneers in the sugar beet and citrus industries while Antone continued to breed Norman-Percheron draft horses as he had done as a young man. Fate smiled on them when some of the orange groves the family planted were needed to build an Air Force base and later, the freeway. Antone was compensated for several rows of mature orange trees at the rate of $1,500 per tree, the value calculated over the tree's projected lifetime. Fortunately for his family, he had planted his rows for quite a distance.

Leo farmed vast acreage in Orange County using methods he'd learned on the Conejo as a boy. Frank acquired land in Imperial and ran a feedlot. The sons acquired land in Arizona, Florida and Texas. By the time the "Santa Ana" Borchards retired in the 1950s, their names were associated with Los Angeles civic arts, banking and charities.

The Borchard brothers and sisters traveled back and forth to spend weekends with each other. When the family grew too large for entertaining in homes, they held family reunions out of doors, sometimes at parks that included the extended family.

The children of Caspar Borchard Sr. were content with their holdings. According to his daughter Teresa, none felt that one had benefited to the detriment of the others. They were happy with each other's successes, prone to offer advice and to learn from each other. They raised their children with respect for the numerous aunts and uncles, and these strong familial ties have endured. Gentleness was a birthright; one generation bequeathing it to another. The family heeded lessons taught by Caspar Borchard Sr. Farming had enough competition from the insects and the weather—it didn't need squabbling among its practitioners. Chance favored the hardest working. There was opportunity enough for all. Cooperation increased the chances for success.

In 1912, Teresa married a distant cousin from the wealthy "Cincinnati Borchards." Edward Valentine Borchard had graduated from Business College and he tackled farming with practicality and innovation. He was an excellent judge of stock. He raised cattle and horses on several thousand acres of owned and leased land while planting over 1200 acres to walnuts and grain. During his stewardship, he farmed his sister-in-law Mary's land as well.

Horses and springtooth on Borchard Ranch. Theresa Kelley and younger sister Rose.

In 1940, Edward V. Borchard retired. Following his death, his sons Robert and Edward formed a partnership with their mother: *The Borchard Brothers Ranch.* Their younger brother Allen joined them when he returned from WW II. Quiet, serious men, they spent much of their time on their tractors and in their fields. Their presence was evident in the summer when the corner of Newbury and Borchard Roads abounded with lush red tomatoes destined for the Hunt Packing Company.

The Borchard Brothers Ranch flourished until 1955, when Edward moved to Salinas. In 1962, Teresa and her sons began selling the land. Eventually Teresa moved from the ranch house where she had lived since her marriage, to a house in Camarillo across the street from her daughter. When failing health required assistance, she lived out her last years until her death at 96, on the site of her old "home place" ranch house, donated for construction of Mary Health of the Sick skilled nursing facility. Her sons moved away to farms in Winters and Salinas, where they continued to grow tomatoes and row crops. They also continued Caspar Sr.'s tradition of raising prize-winning giant pumpkins, often garnering the prize for the world's largest.

During the '40s and '50s, the Borchard brothers employed a watchman of sorts. Harvey was an old man, perhaps a former hired hand who lived as a hermit in an old sheepherder's wagon at the back of their walnut orchard. Harvey became a folk legend, a solitary man who talked to himself and shunned his neighbors. For us children, he made a convincing boogie man with his reed-thin personage, dirty clothes that reeked—or so we imagined. From a safe distance he had a scraggly, gray beard and sharp, piercing eyes.

Every Wednesday morning, promptly at eight, Harvey began his five-mile trek into Newbury Park for groceries. Unless he caught a ride with one of the Borchards, he walked home in the late afternoon, his gunny sack filled with provisions. Summer or winter, his routine never varied.

One early spring afternoon he failed to return home. The nights were still cold enough that the community knew he was in trouble. The brothers combed the area in pickups and on horseback while the sheriff mounted a search and rescue. Neighbor joined neighbor to search. He was found weeks later in the hills behind the Hunt Ranch, dead from exposure. He had apparently become disoriented and wandered off.

Something fundamental seemed to disappear with his passing. For a long time afterward, people watched for him on Wednesday mornings.

The residents along Borchard Road kept an eye out for strangers. It was a long, sparsely populated road and folks knew who belonged. Strangers afoot were escapees from Camarillo State Hospital. Everyone called them "nuts." The first person to spot a walk-away made a phone call to the hospital and another to her nearest neighbor. The phone chain followed the stranger all the way to the highway, warning mothers to gather their children and lock their doors.

Gypsies were another matter. They came each year to Caspar Borchard Sr.'s ranch with women and children perched on the top of a very high bundle of bedding and supplies in the back of a horse-drawn cart. The women undoubtedly kept an eagle eye out for small children, because everyone knew that gypsies would steal them! Caspar Sr. met them on the road, hoping to encourage them to find another spot to camp. The adults engaged him in conversation while the children stole chickens and eggs. When the Gypsy men felt their people had helped themselves to all the watermelons and produce they could get away with, they would congenially shake Caspar Sr.'s hand and move on.

Horses and buggy on the Borchard Ranch

CHAPTER ELEVEN

Coming Together

IN 1888, A widower named John Reily Kelley bought his motherless children from Nebraska and purchased 400 acres of farmland from Caspar Sr. He was a valued and respected member of the community with his beautiful horse, his scientific farming methods and affable offspring. He settled his large family and began raising cattle and hogs on his property near the start of Borchard Road. He rode a big black stallion that people recognized from a distance, and was known to carry gold pieces in his pocket for horse trading.

The family put down long roots. His son Silas married Rosa, my great-grandmother. Caspar Sr. agreed to the marriage. He had great respect for John Reily Kelley and assumed his son would follow in the father's shoes.

For the first few years of their marriage he worked for Caspar Borchard Sr., first in Ojai and then in Talbert, where he and others farmed Borchard land near Huntington Beach. His farming met with limited success when a 100-year flood washed away his crop. In November of that year, he and Rosa welcomed the birth of twins in an isolated house. The following year they were back in the Conejo.

Silas worked hard as a farmer. Later, Caspar Sr.'s thinking centered on a single-minded solution to his son-in-law's economic woes—sheep. A sizable flock could be grazed on the crags and buckhorns that made up the portion of his farm where nothing else would thrive. But Silas was adamant in his hatred of the dumb beasts. For Caspar Sr., Silas' refusal to consider sheep—given that his own flock numbered in the thousands—ground insult into the face of reason.

Other differences divided the two men. Caspar Sr. was a man driven by the need to acquire more and more land. Thrifty and long-sighted, he could see the benefits of hard work and sacrifice. In contrast, Silas was a sociable man. A true son of Ireland, he was a storyteller and a social tippler. People gravitated to him because his blarney brought lighthearted relief to the serious business of living. In another era he might have made his fortune as a salesman. Instead, he was destined to live out his life amid a clan whose values he didn't wholeheartedly embrace.

Silas may not have worked as hard as other farmers of the era, but it wasn't his reputation as a worker that set him at odds with his in-laws. For Caspar Sr. it was worse than that. When John Reily passed away, Silas sold his birthright—land that Caspar Sr. had carved out of his own holdings as a favor. "You never sell land," Caspar Borchard Sr. fumed. "You only buy land." He was afraid that if he left Rosa her share, Silas would sell it as well. In 1913, Caspar Sr., by then a widower, wrote a will that left Rosa's share to her children with a rider guaranteeing her life estate. The next year he revised the will to include a provision that the children must provide financial support for their mother until her death.

The plan worked, more or less. After Silas's death in June 1929, Rosa's support fell mainly to her sons, who sometimes engaged in lively discussions about which of them was doing more. The problems began when the stock market crashed later that year.

When Silas died, Rosa had been married to him for 30 years. She lived another 30 years as his widow. Like her sisters, fate graced her with a long life into her mid eighties. At 78, she still maintained a garden and her hen house, hung her wash and kept a spotless house. She lived frugally and seemed happy with three sons and two daughters still living within hailing distance.

In 1910, the first automobile traveled through the Conejo. Four years later, Silas bought one of the first in the valley and was happy to run errands for his neighbors. In the late 1920s, opportunity took him off the ranch when he was hired by the Ventura County Public Works Department as a construction foreman to supervise the paving of public roads. He excelled at this job. He knew how to work with people; his reputation was that of a fair and enthusiastic boss. His career came to an end, however, when he was abruptly fired and his position given to a more politically connected rancher who coveted a steady paycheck.

Earlier in the decade, Silas had formed a short-lived partnership with a young man named Louie Goeble. Louie had left a privileged life in New York to join the circus and found himself in Los Angeles when the circus wintered there. For a period of time he worked at Universal Studios, cleaning up after the animals until Universal eliminated their wild animal zoo—and with it his job. He purchased a bit of land in Thousand Oaks and brought with him his two lions, Pasha and Queenie. Pasha was the original MGM lion until Leo took his place.

Louie owned lions and Silas owned a truck. Silas traveled around the countryside buying up old or crippled horses to feed to the lions. Probably not something that would be done today, and certainly not in such a public way, but that was another time. It was through this connection that the Olsen children received their first pony.

Louie wanted to get another lion in order to establish a breeding farm in Thousand Oaks, but he lacked the money. He had spent his entire savings, $50, on five lots in the new subdivision of Thousand Oaks. He formed an equal partnership with Silas and they shook hands on it. Unfortunately, Silas had neglected to discuss the matter with his wife. Worse, he failed to mention to her that under the terms of their agreement he would be traveling with the exhibit that Louie had planned until the loan was repaid. Rosa wasn't keen on the idea when she found out. Neither were Silas's sons, who would be expected to handle the farm chores in his absence. The partnership flailed in the light of reason. When Louie was able to come up with the money, he bought out Silas's share.

The Lion Farm became a fixture in Thousand Oaks. Some say it built the town because it gave tourists a reason to seek out the little community with a population of a few hundred, a profusion of live oak trees and predictably balmy weather.

As Louie's finances and reputation grew, he branched out into other exotic animals, which he trained and leased to the movie industry. Eventually he changed the name from *The Lion Farm* to *The World Famous Jungle Compound*. In the 1950s it was sold and renamed *Jungleland*. Among locals it was still referred to as *The Lion Farm*. Whatever its name, *The Lion Farm* was a hard neighbor to ignore. In the '40s, roaring lions could be heard all the way to the Norwegian Colony. From time to time an animal escaped its captivity. Most were recaptured, but a black panther lived out its life in the hills behind Newbury Park, to the consternation of local citizens.

As his fortunes grew, Louie Goeble built a commercial front on his compound that housed a fire department and a burgeoning business center.

Chapter Twelve

Irish Laughter, Irish Tears

It was Silas's damnable luck that Ventura County had become a hotbed for the National Temperance Movement. Photographs of determined women wielding hatchets in front of a Thousand Oaks speakeasy made national front-page news. Once, while Silas and his sons hauled bootleg whiskey out the back door of a distiller's shop, Temperance ladies burst through the front door intent on emptying the inventory onto the street.

It all seems farfetched today, but during the 1920s the country was squaring off either for or against imbibers. Few people were undecided. Silas Kelley's fondness for a good time created discord among his wife's family, who were strident non-drinkers. Rosa remained loyal to her husband and could probably see both sides of the argument; it was in the presence of lubricious companionship that Silas flourished.

Silas was an inordinately popular man and his children took pride in him. In later years his sons drove him to speakeasies, drank alongside him—and in the wee hours of the morning brought him home again, happy and probably in trouble with their mother. When he occasionally disappeared for a few days at the end of harvest season, Rosa spent her days among her chickens and turkeys until he returned. It must have put her in an untenable position, living within sight of her father and having to listen to his opinions. There was little privacy for the couple to settle their differences. Whenever Silas failed to return home after a night of merry making, and his car was missing from its customary parking spot, Rosa's brothers knew to drop by to milk the cows and feed the pigs.

Tracy's brothers' exploits were legendary. They raced horses—and later, model T's and roadsters. They stayed out late, caroused on Saturday nights and managed to ruffle the feathers of their reserved aunts and uncles up the road. Uncle Ed Borchard was not amused when a couple of his Kelley nephews cut the tip off his cigar, filled it with dirt and fastened the top back on to watch as he tried unsuccessfully to get a draw.

In the Irish tradition, the Kelley children were numerous.

Charlie was the oldest, a quiet man who lived with his mother and never married. He subscribed to the *Los Angeles Times* and let his nephews read the Sunday funnies. He was drafted into WWI, but avoided service when the war ended while he was still in training camp. He loved to fish and drove often to the beach. He supported his widowed mother and built her a new house on property he had inherited from his Borchard grandfather.

Charlie worked for the Janss Ranch in the era of dryland bean farming, and usually got assigned the dangerous jobs that none of the married men wanted. After he quit, Charlie worked as a maintenance man for Ventura County. He spent his last day crawling inside huge tanks and cleaning them out with carbon tetra-chloride. Later that night he suffered a fatal heart attack. It wasn't until others suffered the same fate that doctors made a connection and the government enacted new regulations for the chemical.

Theresa, my grandmother, was serious, thrifty and hard working. As the oldest girl, she helped her mother with a brood of boys reared under a freer set of rules. She loved people and thrived on entertaining.

John, Theresa's twin, had handsome dark eyes and mischievous smile. Even the jaunty tilt to his hat indicated his outlook on life. He loved horses, a pipe and Prince Albert tobacco, his children and telling a good story. He farmed, and for many years was the genial Conejo School bus driver.

Walter was a wag who loved a good party. He ran a dairy and hired many of his nephews and prospective brothers-in-law as milkers. He seemed garrulous and stern by turns to me as a child. Like his father, he drank, but he could be counted on to protect his mother and his sisters. In his mid-30s he married Helga. He met her when he delivered milk to her as a new widow, after her husband was killed when his automobile collided with an oak tree at the corner of Moorpark Road where modern-day Oaks Shopping Mall sits. He was childless until Helga's grown son knocked on their door one day, a secret she had kept lest he find out that she was nine years older and previously divorced. But apparently her fears were for naught because they lived together happily into old age. She in fact outlived him by 18 years.

Within the family he was the keeper of the flame. When his sister Rose traveled to Oregon in search of a cure for her cancer, Walter went along and cared for her. He kept up her spirits and relayed news of the family while he sought treatment for his asthma at the same time.

Fred Sr. was the youngest boy, smart, social and easy going. He laughed easily and seemed more relaxed. As a boy, the highpoint of his week was driving the farm wagon to Oxnard each week for groceries purchased at Cohn's in El Rio. The trip began in the early morning, after the cows were milked, and ended late in the afternoon before chores needed to be done. Everything had to be bought in Oxnard, and the trip was taken by horse and wagon, rain or shine. As an adult, Fred lived a stone's throw from his mother's house and served as the Fire Chief at Port Hueneme Naval Base. He was also the last surviving Kelley brother on the Conejo. He and his wife Mildred bought a saloon along the old boardwalk in Nevada City. Later they moved to Arroyo Grande. When Mildred passed, he moved back to the home place where he lived for the rest of his life. Intelligent and quiet spoken, a good family man, he lacked the flamboyance of his brothers, but his intelligence was his bequest to his children and grandchildren. All three of his sons, Bobby, Billy and Fred Jr., continued to live in the Conejo, Bobby until his death at an early age.

Rose was a dark-eyed Irish beauty, whose life seemed surrounded in tragedy. She was tall and lovely, the mother of three boys. Her husband Harry was a carpenter. He built houses for William Randolph Hearst in Cambria before they returned to the Conejo. Her son Ralph was a young boy when an unfortunate accident claimed the life of his brother, two-year-old Donnie.

One of their neighbors, the Louie Goebles, owned a pet panther that was kept chained on a vacant lot. Donnie was returning from his grandmother's house on the other side of the vacant lot, carrying a fresh cookie in his hands. He put the cookie in his mouth and tried to pet the panther, but it swiped the cookie, tearing the boy's throat with its sharp claws. His father Harry drove him to St. John's Hospital in Oxnard while Rose cradled him in her arms. Three days later he died and was buried on his third birthday.

Donnie Fletcher with his mother Rose.

Rose was pregnant at the time. Her son Patrick was born six months later. It was said that she was diagnosed with breast cancer while in her early pregnancy, but she opted to carry the child and to breastfeed him afterward to give him a healthy start. By the time she sought medical treatment it was too late. She was 36 when she passed away in Ashland, Oregon.

Her husband eventually married Olga, a widow with a young son, Sandy. Olga seemed to resist the forced association with the Kelley clan, who grieved their beloved sister. One of her sisters-in-law recalled receiving a Christmas gift intended for Patrick, her godchild. It was returned from Olga, unopened with an explanation that Rose's boys could not accept a gift unless her own son received one as well.

When Harry died, Rose's property transferred to his second wife. When Olga passed, her legal will left her entire estate to her natural son, Sandy. Rose's sons got none of their mother's land.

Dorothy was a sweet, gentle girl, stylish and creative, who married a Cajun man that her cousin met at a cockfight and brought home for dinner. She was a good sport, clever and hard working. She attended beauty school in San Pedro and opened a beauty shop in one of Louie Goeble's commercial units next to the fire department. As the family's first career woman, Dorothy gave her nieces "Shirley Temple" perms and shared Conejo news with her stay-at-home sisters when they dropped by to visit. She closed up shop for a year to follow her husband Earl to San Pedro during WW II. When he shipped out on the USS Oklahoma to Pearl Harbor, she returned and reopened the shop.

On the day after the Japanese bombed the harbor and the Oklahoma was sunk, Tracy, her brother Fred and their families heard the news on the radio. They invented an excuse to spend the afternoon with Dorothy in case she received bad news, but they agreed ahead of time that no one would tell her about the bombing until after they ate. Over a half-century later, Fred's son, Fred Jr., remembered that he blurted it out in the middle of supper. His Aunt Dorothy had to be revived from a swoon and he received the bawling out of his life.

Dorothy was forced to wait for three days until her husband's cockfighting friend told her he had located Earl in a hospital, safe and recovering from a back injury. She waited several weeks before the government sent a letter and even longer before her husband's heavily censored letter finally arrived explaining that he was found unconscious on a beach after swimming ashore through oily water. He had been hospitalized after jumping over the side of the battleship into a safety boat with burning oil all around him. He escaped burns but sustained injuries to his back that plagued him through his life. After four months of recuperation he was reassigned to the Pacific.

Earl added a layer of color to the family tree with his Cajun looks and enthusiasm for making money in any manner except farming. After his retirement from the Navy, he returned home to resume a lucrative cockfighting business, raising his roosters in a sheltered nook on his wife's property. In the 1950s they sold their Conejo home and moved to a secluded ranch property in Arroyo Grande.

When Dorothy lay dying of stomach cancer in the City of Hope hospital, in Los Angeles, her brother Walter stayed in a boarding house connected with the hospital. Her family visited regularly, but he remained at her side until she died so that she wouldn't be alone.

Josephine, ebony-haired and Irish fey, was the vivacious youngest. She had an infectious laugh, was prone to seeing spirits and ghosts, including the one that lived in her mother Rosa's house. She liked to accompany herself on the guitar on summer evenings, singing cowboy songs. She and her husband Cyril worked as psychiatric technicians at Camarillo State Hospital and had a lifetime of interesting adventures. She made a wicked batch of thin fudge that we called "runny," that has kept her memory as close as our pantry.

The siblings' ages spanned so many years that the two younger girls, Dorothy and Josephine, had their babies at the same ages as their nieces. The result was an assortment of first and second cousins that created confusion for the teachers at Timber School, where four generations of Borchards and Kelleys attended through the years. Children understood the difference between a first and a second cousin. The distinction affected invitations to parties, the style of clothing they could afford and the gossip that drifted to little ears. At Christmas time, the great-grandchildren watched as Grandma Kelley gave her grandchildren their Christmas gifts. Rosa always had a plastic stocking filled with candy and oranges for each of us. Regardless of the fact that we celebrated our big Christmas the following night, we always envied the Kelley cousins. But our mother reminded us that we had another set of first cousins and they had only each other.

We envied those who carried the family name. My father's name, Thompson, seemed plain and undistinguished. It obscured my claim to Kelleyness. I wondered how Tracy felt when she changed her name to Olsen. Family names were used and reused. If babies weren't christened with their aunt's or uncle's first names, they often carried them as a middle name. A name was a way of tying the generations together, of honoring both the newborn and the original. My mother offended Tracy by dropping the 'h' in my first name, Teresa, and insisting that I be called by my middle name. In the throes of the 60's Social Revolution, I dropped the tradition, but fortunately my cousin Helen kept us on track when she named her daughter Theresa.

The clan of cousins was close-knit. Most of them were born in the 1920s and '30s, when the isolation of the Conejo forced them to share almost every facet of their lives—a tribe of cousins that grew up within hailing distance from each other. Tracy's son Neil was the exception. His visits to the Kelley clan were fraught with the same practical jokes and teasing that his father had endured a generation earlier. Neil stayed at his Grandmother Kelley's house on only three occasions. As a boy he had to stick close to the house whenever he visited because his mother wanted him to avoid bad influences. He had little in common with his Irish cousins and didn't inherit their jovial outlook.

The Kelley siblings were heart and soul, involved in each other's lives. In later years, their recollections were peppered with stories of each other and their first cousins. Their lives had been an extension of their parents, their stories filled with craziness and boldness, daring and freedom that seemed inconceivable to later generations. Sometimes it seemed like a miracle that they survived their childhoods.

Tracy's brothers probably thought she was dour. She possessed a serious, critical side, probably a result of shouldering too much responsibility at an early age. Her mother's experience had imbued in her distrust for fraternizing men. When she looked around for a husband, the admonition that "he drinks" was enough to dismiss a young man from consideration. In Tracy's eyes, how much or how little a man consumed wasn't the point. A bad habit had the potential to lie dormant for many months or years before it exploded, most likely when a husband's pockets were filled with cash from the sale of summer beef. Oscar fit her criteria. He held to his promise never to take a drink. Throughout their marriage they substituted tea, Watkin's orange concentrate, or lemonade made with lemons from their own yard.

My sisters and brothers inherited a mix of Irish and Norwegian disposition. Even as children we admired the way our Irish great-uncles livened up our family picnics. Red-faced and garrulous, they could be counted on to hire a bagpiper and dance a jig. When they told their stories, children sat nearby and tried to appear not to be listening so that our mothers wouldn't whisk us away.

Celebrations were held outdoors with picnic tables made of sawhorses and barn planks. Tables were piled high with potluck, including Rosa Kelley's famous German potato salad. In the early years, tables were set up in her yard, beneath a huge valley oak and a towering *Washingtonia* palm. Whenever the Borchards arrived for a family reunion, the party moved to Oak Grove Park, at the base of the Conejo Grade, and opened up to all the family, a hundred or more Borchards, Kelleys, Freidrichs, Olsens, Colwells, Ashbys, Maulhardts and assorted others. Except for the Santa Ana Borchards, few had to travel more than 20 miles to attend.

Walter would lead some of the fellows on surreptitious trips to the front seat of his battered green pickup, after which the tempo of the party would pick up. Usually he offered my sisters a quarter to sing "You Are My Sunshine," which we sang in three-part harmony while attempting to avoid our mother's frown. Mama felt we should refuse the money offered by an inebriated man. In her opinion, Walter offered a poor example. One year he got boisterous and engaged his brother in a wrestling match. The two middle-aged men butted and backed each other to the ground while we children watched with saucer-sized eyes.

The Kelley boys told ear-popping stories. They knew how the great men came upon their fortunes, or lost their fortunes, or got bucked off a cantankerous horse into the cactus. They had stories of philandering husbands and women no better than they had to be, and fainting women who had to be dragged out of church and revived. They shared stories of great cattle drives and cowboy movie stars who had to be taught to ride. A cousin who taught child stars at MGM on the set. Every family picnic and gathering centered around the table where the three Kelley brothers sat. Their brand of humor was hearty. In a crowd of people, a Kelley—brother or sister—could be recognized by the sound of their laughter. I thought my great-aunts and uncles were wonderful.

In later years stories of imbibing proved to be mostly hearsay. Walter might decide to drive home, but someone took his keys and the matter was settled. John might have yearned to join him, but his wife Babe would have none of the nonsense. Fred never drank. By the early 1960s, Silas had died of heart trouble. Charlie had taken "the cure" a decade before his death. John died of leukemia. Only Walter and Fred remained.

John inherited his father's charm and gift of storytelling. Babe kept him on the straight and narrow. We children loved him. He was handsome, kind and clever, a magnet for friends. He imbued every gathering with a sense of fun. Photos of him as a young man show a slim, self-assured man with the same intense gaze as actor Sam Elliott. He rode a horse well and had a habit of doffing his western hat by the crown and lifting it in a sweeping gesture with a jaunty tilt and an enthusiastic "Yippeeee!" It was that gesture that first caught the attention of the young woman who would later become his wife.

He and a cousin, Bertha, stood up for Oscar and Tracy at their wedding. Babe might have served as bridesmaid, but she was still in high school. They married as soon as she finished school in Fallbrook.

Babe's legal name was Olive, although only her teachers called her that. To everyone else she was "Babe," the nickname given her by her father on the day of her birth. Photos of her as a young girl show a self-assured, athletic girl who loved tennis. She was a member of California's first Girl Scouts troop, which Julia Lowe, the founder of the Girl Scouts, visited when she came west. Babe raised three fiercely independent children, all high achievers. She sent her daughter Catherine to the University of California at Los Angeles. My mother called Babe "a woman ahead of her time."

Babe's mother had been married to a man who left for long periods to the Klondike. When gold eluded him, he earned his living toting equipment and supplies a hundred pounds at a time, on his back over the daunting Chilkoot Trail. After an absence of seven years he returned to his wife, who had no inkling of whether he was alive or not. She declared that if he ever left again she would divorce him. He did. And true to her word, she did as well. She later married a man who did contract butchering for Caspar Borchard Sr. from his butcher shop in Hueneme. They met when he rode his bicycle to Hollywood to buy lemons from her citrus orchard. Either he had heard about the pretty divorcee or he had a terrific yen for lemons.

After Babe's mother died of cancer, her father fostered her out to a Mexican family with eight children. She loved being a part of a large family. When one of the younger girls became pregnant, Babe's father decided it wasn't a fit environment for his daughter and placed her with a childless, older couple who doted on her. She lived with them until she married.

John and Babe seemed more sophisticated than the rest of the family. Babe was a great talker who was infinitely more young-at-heart than the other women around her. She was a disinterested cook who did so only when the urge struck. If her husband arrived home and no meal was ready, he cooked supper. John was in the habit of wearing his hat everywhere. He was one of a generation of men with a white band across his forehead where his skin never saw sunlight. In later years, Babe liked to tell that he wouldn't even answer the door without donning his hat.

Their son Michael was a Veterinarian with a photographic memory, who met his wife Merrie at vet school. Together they opened their practice, Cottage Hospital, a vet clinic and surgery center for animals. Daughter Catherine served as a State Department translator and international educator. Another son, John Jr., was a successful horse trainer, farrier and horse broker, despite being confined to a wheelchair from his late twenties. The family was devastated when John Sr. died at 59 of leukemia. Babe lived in their family home on Borchard Road until she sold and moved to Somis, near her son. She passed in her 90s.

With the G.I. Bill, farmers' sons started going to college and the family seemed filled with bright young minds. The success of one member seemed to validate the rest of the family. Higher education paved the way to having all the things that had been unattainable growing up and everyone wanted a part of it. A lot of us farm kids had had it with green grass and quiet sunsets. We wanted to try chaos and city life with all the trappings. But we wanted to bring our children home to the family farm for holidays and summer breaks.

Fred Kelley Jr. earned his engineering degree at U.C. Berkeley and traveled the world as an engineer, but he served his apprenticeship at his Uncle Walter's dairy farm. At age 7 he learned to drive Walter's hay truck. After his eighth birthday, he milked 18 cows on the weekends when Walter's regular milker had time off. Two milkings a day. For this he earned 75 cents for the weekend. After the morning milking he helped run the bottled milk route with Walter, taking five and ten gallon cans of milk to the creamery in Ventura. After the afternoon milking he bottled milk and separated cream. When his brother Bill turned 8, he joined Fred in milking. Fred's son, Fred Kelley III, earned an M.D. in bio-medical physics and maintains a career in Public Health. Presumably he knows how to milk a cow.

Five generations. From rear: John Kelley Sr., Theresa Kelley Olsen, Rosa Kelley. Caspar Borchard Sr. holding great- granddaughters Catherine and Arthelia.

CHAPTER THIRTEEN

Lessons Learned

MANY FIFTH-GENERATION Borchards, Kelleys and Olsens remain connected to the land. They have chosen careers as managers of corporate farms, horsemen, managers of ranches like the Wood Ranch in Simi, as agricultural chemical spray consultants, nutritionists. They are professionals whose work reflects their farm roots. Some were fortunate enough to inherit land from their parents and continue farming with an unbroken seam. Before they took over control of their family farms, many earned a degree from an agricultural college like Davis or Cal Poly, San Luis Obispo.

Today, education is an essential part of agriculture. Sons come home from college and argue progressive methods with their fathers the way Caspar Sr. and Silas Kelley argued about sheep. Their success will be more elusive than it was for our great-grandfathers who lived in the brief period of American farming when land was cheap, labor was plentiful and a strong dollar and wartime needs paid well for crops that could be shipped long distances. Caspar Borchard Sr. and his neighbors made use of apprenticeship, common sense and shared knowledge. Their great-grandsons use computers, accountants and genetic technology. If they could have a conversation with the old men of the Conejo, the present day farmers would undoubtedly hold their own.

The sound of Irish argument still stirs the evening breeze along Borchard Road. If one hears voices of old farmers raised in passionate discourse, it might be the Borchard or the Kelley brothers clustered around a celestial dinner table. The luxury of being able to strongly disagree belongs to families who know each other well.

Makeshift housing dotted the Conejo during the first part of the century. Construction sheet rock didn't exist until after WW II. Until then, the walls of marginal houses called "shacks" were a single layer of wood. Single men lived in bunkhouses. Most everyone else lived on their farms until towns slowly began to develop. A few wealthy farmers built houses that would last through the ages. The rest built what they could afford

In the Conejo the first shacks were stud-wall skeletons of redwood 2x4's covered on the outside with 12-inch redwood siding that shrank as the wood aged so that drafts blew through the cracks. Batten siding nailed over the seams helped, but didn't prevent field dust from filtering into a housewife's flour and beans, even face powder. In the closets, two layers of wood provided a pocket into which a housewife could stuff newspapers to provide a crude insulation. Newspaper attracted rats and mice. When the odor of rodents became noticeable, walls and floors were sometimes taken up and the newspaper insulation was replaced. Housewives stretched cheesecloth or very thin muslin over interior stud walls. The lucky ones then glued wallpaper onto the cloth with wheat-flour paste. But they complained that the walls flexed with every passing breeze.

John Kelley Sr.'s first house was just such a shack, rented in what is now Wildwood Park. The door latch was broken and the landlord didn't see any need to fix it. John and Babe propped an Indian bowl against the door to keep it closed against snakes and skunks. In their second house in Ventu Park, Babe's aunt came to visit and watched in horror as several insects scuttled beneath a sheet of peeled-back wallpaper. She declared that the house was infested with bedbugs. Babe's father-in-law, Silas, when he heard about it, teased his young daughter-in-law by telling her that bedbugs would chew the ears off of her babies. Babe had a baby in bed only inches from the wall.

Silas allowed that kerosene would kill most anything that crawled. Ignorant of its dangers, Babe sent her young husband to Camarillo to pick up kerosene. The two of them painted it onto the wallpaper, onto the floors, the attic and the doors. They poured some into small cans and set them beneath the baby's bed. In the evening they lit their kerosene lanterns and proceeded to go about their routine. As an old lady, Babe considered it a miracle that they didn't burst into flames.

Their oldest son, John Jr. (Johnny), cowboyed for the Janss Ranch in the early 1950s. He later roped for the Hearsts, near present-day Westlake Village. He was an amateur boxer in the El Rio boxing rings, a horseshoer, cowboy, roper and bull rider. He won All-Around Cowboy at the Ventura County Fair in 1949. His son John III (Nonnie), won the same award 20 years later. One night John Jr. awoke, partially paralyzed. Even among his best friends, the stories differ. Some say he injured his back picking up the tongue of a horse trailer. For four years he experienced increasing pain as he worked as a horseshoer and pursued the rodeo circuit with an eye to a national title. He suffered his final injury when a horse fell on him while riding.

Eventually he was forced to choose between possible total paralysis and risky back surgery. He elected for surgery in hopes the damage could be corrected. He came out of the operation paralyzed from the neck down. Through months of therapy he saw slow improvement as the paralysis receded from his neck, slowly down his chest. Eventually he regained full motion of his arms and torso.

The community rallied to Johnny's aid with a fundraising barbecue arranged by his roping buddy, Fire Chief Tom Moody. Others stepped up: dairywoman Belle Holloway—for whom he had once "hopped" milk bottles to home customers—and Ralph Hays, a cousin who owned Oxnard Plumbing and Roofing, where Johnny worked as foreman. The population of the Conejo at the time was around 2,000 people. Most of them attended the barbecue and ate beef donated by Joel McCrea, the Borchard Brothers and the Janss Corporation. The newspaper noted that everything was donated except the paper plates.

Johnny couldn't attend his party; his doctors wouldn't discharge him from the hospital for another three months. His friends and neighbors covered many of his medical expenses. They stayed his friends for life. His wife Alta was a beautiful woman with Indian blood, who wore her black hair pulled back like an Indian princess. She coped with grace and generosity in a situation that irretrievably altered her life as well.

When the despair lifted, Johnny began to salvage his options for a future that held little promise of the intense activity he loved. Told that hydrotherapy would be helpful, he sketched out a design for a swimming pool on a piece of paper. Friends dug a pit in his front yard, framed it with wooden forms and rebar, and poured a concrete swimming pool with a ramp at one end so he could roll himself in and out of the water in his wheelchair. He rigged a driving harness to lift himself into a station wagon that he drove using very early hand controls.

When he was able to return to work, Johnny trained horses, rode fence lines in his vehicle and brokered cattle and horses. He retained his sense of humor. Like his father, his storytelling was legendary. Sometimes, instead of doing their homework, his sons hid behind the sofa in their small living room and listened into the wee hours to his stories of the Conejo. His sons Bill, John III, and Ralph were his legacy; they figured out the really important things in life before they got sidetracked. Watching someone triumph over adversity was a gift from God. As children, his sons absorbed lessons that I'm not sure Johnny knew he was teaching.

———————

Dryland farmers and stockmen are a stoic breed. They can be identified from across a room. When a joke is told, when the weather has turned and the grass is dry, sometimes the best they can manage is smile that doesn't quite reach the eye. When a bull gets tied up in barbed wire and has to be sold for slaughter, stockmen take out their frustration in a burst of hard work. They go off by themselves for hours, maybe days, building fences or laying in a crop of hay while they try to make sense of their vulnerability. Maybe they don't recognize it as fear, but as a pervasive sense of fatalism. Dryland farmers don't let themselves get too happy or too discouraged. It is their nature to hold something always in reserve.

When a dryland farmer looks out at his fields and sees a thick carpet of green poking through the sodden earth, he doesn't laugh at his good fortune. Too much can go wrong before the harvest. When his grain is knee-high and bowed with the weight of its barley heads, he casts an eye at the rain clouds and listens for thunder. He worries about a stray cigarette tossed out along the fence line that borders the road. When the harvest is gathered into his granaries for the winter, he feels contentment in the year's efforts. He wipes the dust from his boots, takes his wife to the neighborhood dance and potluck supper, talks yields and prices with anyone who will listen. He may take a day off to visit the county fair. Then he starts to worry about the coming year again.

By the same measure, if grasshoppers eat his seed or the sun crusts the soil so that the seed can't germinate, if rains don't come and grass is half what he needs to hold his herd over the winter, he recalls the contentment of a full harvest. The memory keeps him going. A farmer can't let himself get flat-out happy. He has already paid for the good times and he knows he will suffer the bad times again.

Stockmen are the same. They settle for contentment, living life on their own terms. It is a life they wouldn't trade for anything on earth. They seldom voice this feeling to outsiders, and maybe not even to themselves. It is caught in the updrafts of air currents that stir the grasses, in the cicadas that fly through the evening haze. A man's contentment resonates in the way he calls to his wife, "Come quick," to share the 'v' flight pattern of mallards and geese flying south in the fall; the shared experience as meaningful to the rancher as a bottle of vintage Chardonnay on a wine merchant's shelf.

When a child grows up surrounded by a family of dryland farmers like the Borchards, that child might wonder if they were born without a gene that allows them to be outrageous. This was what Silas brought into the family. The Kelleys weren't as stoic as the Borchards or the Olsens. They didn't hold anything in reserve.

CHAPTER FOURTEEN

Sisters and Daughters

SILAS KELLEY DIED in the spring of 1929, leaving Rosa with a life insurance policy. Rosa deposited it along with her father's inheritance, totaling more than $10,000, in the Thousand Oaks Savings and Loan, an up-and-coming investment institution. Her sister Mary did the same with her own inheritance.

The stock market crashed in October of that year. Shortly afterward the Savings and Loan went bankrupt. Rosa's family rallied around her. In the aftermath of her loss her sons wrote letters, made trips to the Ventura County seat, joined others urging legislative investigations, but nothing produced results. The money had disappeared as surely as her hopes for a comfortable old age. The FDIC Insurance Program didn't come into effect until after the financial collapse, and it wouldn't have covered savings and loans, anyway. Investors were out of luck.

Rosa Kelley lived the rest of her life with regret. Her son Charlie remained at home and provided for his mother. After Charlie's death, Walter took over farming his mother's land and paid her a sum for its use so that she had spending money.

By the mid-1950s, Rosa was in her 80s and needed live-in help. Florence Hays, an area pioneer, was hired to care for her, with her children sharing the cost. Their mother's needs were simple. She had kept Silas's car for her children to use on her errands. When it finally wore out she did not replace it.

Rosa's sister Mary lost her savings as well, but she retained her land. Her brother-in-law farmed it, but she made many of the decisions. Oscar's cancelled checks included a check made out in 1927 to Mary Borchard, for $7.50. The memo line indicated, "seed grain."

Mary remained with her father, keeping house for the two of them in a two-story farm house that stood along Borchard Park. After his death she had a small house built behind Teresa and Edward's house so she could be a part of her sister's growing family of three boys and two girls. Teresa never learned to sew, so Mary made the children's clothing, mended and did the laundry.

Mary owned a '38 Packard and drove her two sisters on their errands. Extraordinarily thrifty and practical, she was probably wealthier than her brothers, yet she worked like a maid. She died a millionaire, but she cut down her old dresses to make her petticoats and underwear, and poured her strong coffee into a saucer to cool it before she sipped it from the saucer. Sharp-tongued at times, she seemed stern when compared to her sisters Rosa and Teresa, but she lived as a model of self-sacrifice and dedication.

Aunt Mary was especially kind to my mother. When Mary moved from her father's old home, she gave the two-story farmhouse to my father for salvage. In doing so she bucked the advice of her brother-in-law Edward, who wanted to sell the house for a good sum. My father used the wood to build a small rental house on Charles Street in Moorpark, a washroom for my mother, a playhouse for us and many cabinets and interior walls. Most of the boards were 1x12's sawn from old-growth redwood, dense, clear and often 20 feet long.

The last time Aunt Mary drove it was to visit my mother. She brought vegetables and cuttings from her garden and stayed for lunch. As she got into her car to drive the mile and a half back to her house she became confused and had to ask directions. She never drove again.

She died in 1965, at age 87, at St. John's Nursing Home, in Oxnard, shortly after Mary Health of the Sick was built on land that she and her sister donated to the nuns for a care facility.

———————

Tracy quit high school after her sophomore year to help at home while her mother underwent treatment for breast cancer. Rosa mentioned in a letter to her sister-in-law that she had developed a lump. Her Santa Ana sisters-in-law arrived in their automobile, packed her up and took her back to Los Angeles for treatment, to a woman who could cure cancer with a poultice that drew tumors from the body. They visited the woman at her home in Culver City and watched as she made a poultice in a flannel wrap. She tied it under Grandma's arm, near her lymph gland, wrapped her in a tight bandage and settled her in bed. The bandage was changed frequently and new herbs and poultice added. Within a period of months the tumor disappeared. Rosa returned home and lived to be 85 years old.

In later years the cancer story took on a sort of "wives tale" element and was relegated to the "we won't speak of it" category. Fifty years later, Mary Olsen Rydberg interviewed an old woman, Mrs. Miller, about her pioneer memories of Minnesota. Mrs. Miller mentioned that she had known a woman who cured cancer, "with a poultice that drew the thing right out of the skin, feelers and all." Mrs. Miller claimed they lost touch when the healer moved to Los Angeles.

While her mother was gone, Tracy held the fort at home. Her sisters were 12, 16 and 18 years younger than she was and their father never expected them to work like Tracy had done at their age. In later years, Oscar often claimed that he married her to get her out of the house.

As a bride she probably stood on the stoop of her brand new house, relieved to be spared the responsibilities. She didn't miss the rough-and-tumble days on the Kelley Ranch when her brothers occupied the bachelor wing of the upstairs farmhouse and clumped downstairs for supper. She learned her skills at an early age cooking huge meals for brothers, cousins and hired men. In later years, her aunts told stories of how hard she worked, cooking and washing for everyone in the family.

The house Tracy grew up in was a thin-walled two-story, built by a shirttail relative. Like in most farmhouses of the era, the ground floor was primarily kitchen and pantry. A built-in bench along one side of the table accommodated unexpected meal guests, the number of which varied with the harvest season. The bedrooms were small and unheated. Later, her brother Charlie had a more modern home built. It was smaller, but sounder, with two bedrooms and a parlor.

Behind the main house, the men built a bunkhouse intended for the hired hands. It became a haven for Tracy's brothers and cousins looking for independence from their fathers. The boys slept, gambled, played their guitars and lounged around with bachelor impunity, coming into the main house only for meals. Single men bunked at the ranch while they worked day jobs on harvesting crews, hoeing beans or working sheep and cattle during the teens and twenties. As strictly bachelor quarters it was out-of-bounds to females, even though the girls would sometimes peek inside then run off before they could be caught and punished. The room was furnished with a solid row of beds and a straight-back chair or two.

As was the custom in those days, the Kelley boys lived in the bunkhouse for free while they worked at surrounding ranches for pay.

Others paid a token fee for board and room from their wages. Tracy worked without compensation.

———

Fair womanhood seems to have engendered inequality among its Conejo maidens. To a startling degree, the ease of a woman's existence depended on the man she chose for her mate. Those who chose poorly served as a cautionary lesson to their nieces. The vagaries of fate courted some and teased others. Borchard women expected to live long lives; they needed good husbands who would provide for growing Catholic families.

In the days of cheap and abundant manual labor, a greater division of roles existed between man and woman. Rosa Kelley and her sisters were left to tend huge gardens and to perform traditional tasks throughout a brutally long workday that included bearing and tending children. Theirs was a steady diet of mundane, often unfulfilling tasks spanning from daylight to bedtime, while men worked in spurts, seasonally, often from the back of a horse or vehicle. However, most women were not expected to do heavy tasks. Should a woman need her wash water heated and hauled, it was her husband, son or hired man who saw to the task. The young boys usually turned the crank on the washing machine to run it through the wringer for rinsing. Should anything go amiss, a man was usually within hailing distance. Ladies remained in the house and yard, men in the field. But farm life held enough work for everyone, man or woman.

The Borchard sisters enjoyed a close-knit sisterhood. One might drop in at any time with recipes, an apron pattern or her delicious German coffee cake—thin slabs of sweet yeast dough covered with thick cream and sugar, baked to golden custard and sprinkled with cinnamon. A pan could disappear in a trice when hungry boys passed through the kitchen and cut themselves a generous slice.

Sisters and cousins visited each other and often stayed for a meal. Sometimes they stayed overnight and helped each other put up peaches when the fruit ripened, or sewed a wedding dress, or nursed a sick child through the night.

When their mother died, the Borchard sisters learned to depend upon themselves. They dispensed advice, worried about their hands and the effects of the sun on their complexions. They looked out for each other's children, and when the time came, some made their wills with nephews and nieces in mind.

Any woman who made an unfortunate marriage found herself wanting as she grew older. Her lot didn't improve with age, especially for childless woman like Silas's sister, Elizabeth. Aunt Lizzy, as she was called, had been abandoned or divorced by a husband in Texas years before, and made her way back to the Conejo where she had grown up. For as long as she was able, Lizzy worked as a ranch cook for Ida and Caspar Borchard Jr. As she got older, Aunt Lizzy suffered from nerves, possibly agoraphobia, and seldom left her house.

Her house was a one-room shack with 144 square feet of living space, including a lean-to kitchen with a kerosene two-burner stove and a bit of board for a work counter. A boardwalk of loose, mismatched boards connected the house to an outhouse. The shack was perched in a hollow off of Ventu Park Road, on the other side of a dry creekbed. In the winter, rains swelled the creek and isolated Lizzy from the town. In the muddy season it was a challenge for drivers to get their cars up to speed to cross the creek in order to bring her supplies. Many valley residents claimed a relationship to Aunt Lizzy by marriage or by circumstance. Whoever was passing by brought kerosene and ice for her icebox, produce from their gardens or staples from the market. When someone butchered, a portion of meat was set aside for her.

Every year or two, Lizzy's sister Minny would arrive from Arizona with a small carpetbag containing her entire wardrobe—two fancy black beaded dresses, possibly some rich woman's cast-offs from the turn-of-the century. Her wardrobe never varied. She still owned the same two taffeta dresses, or others similar, when she died in the 1940s. Hopelessly outdated and covered with elaborate beading, they were museum pieces even at the time she wore them.

One year the county paid Lizzy fifteen dollars a month to take in two teenage girls who needed a place to live. Lizzy and Minnie—and any visitor who happened by for the day to bring supplies and news—sat on the beds and did needlework or quilted while their children played in the dirt outside.

In an era without employment insurance, people worked for as long as they were able. Widows cooked for harvest crews to support their children. Old men who ended up land wealthy boasted of their early days hopping bottles for dairies, poisoning gophers and squirrels for ranchers, hoeing beans on dryland ranches, picking and pitting apricots, doing a variety of temporary and long-term jobs that provided a living. Resumes were unheard of in those days; a friendly word and a handshake were all that was needed. People depended on each other to help out, bumper crops or bust. Social Security was a concept that came along too late for all the Aunt Lizzies of the era. No matter. The two women were sisters of Silas Kelley. People looked out for their own.

In the Conejo, fortune did not favor all its inhabitants with a steady hand. Only a few years before Silas drove his automobile around the valley, his brother John Reily Kelley Jr. and his wife Lucy were married in Los Angeles. They made their way to Oklahoma in a covered wagon. She was known to everyone as Aunt Lucy. The two of them came to California in the 1890s from Oklahoma before returning to Texas. They made a trip to visit, in the same covered wagon pulled by a team of sturdy horses, searching for a way to make a living for their family of six. In the course of their travels the family increased to ten children.

In visits to the Kelley sisters, Aunt Lucy recalled living all over Texas and Oklahoma, mounted Indians watching them from mesas as their wagon rolled along at the pace set by their worn-out horses. She remembered that the horses were not good travelers because they lacked stamina and suffered from thirst more than mules, but they were cheaper to purchase. For better or worse, horses were the best they could afford. On one trip, Aunt Lucy carried two barrels of yeast starter for making bread. When their water barrels ran dry she fed her thirsty children the slurry that contained enough water to sustain them until they reached the next water source. The memory of that yeast made it a comfort food for her. She craved it for the rest of her life.

They arrived at Long Beach, desperately poor and starving. One of the children managed to bring down a seagull, the only food at hand, with a stone. Plucked, the bird's flesh was black and rubbery. They tried roasting it over a small fire they built on the sand, but even cooked, the gull was so tough that when they threw it to the dogs, the dogs ignored it.

Years earlier on his trip west, Caspar Borchard Sr.'s uncle Christian was involved in an incident that haunted him throughout his lifetime. His dog killed an Indian that attacked his covered wagon, probably for food. He seldom spoke of it and bitterly regretted the accident because he did not wish to be known for this one deed. When pressed to tell the story, he let it be inferred that his big black dog chased the marauding Indian away.

One of the other Kelley sisters, Melissa, was married to a handsome, cocky Texas cowboy, Joe Buchard. He left in search of ranch work and never was heard from again. She later remarried and raised her family. In 1938, Aunt Lucy was seventy years old. Her spirit and her stories live in the memories of her great-grand nephews and nieces, and even in those who could claim no relationship except by association. Sad to think that the next generation of *Aunt Lucys* has vaporized in the social isolation of modern day America.

––––––––––

The connection from Caspar Borchard Sr.'s generation to present day is not merely a connection of the land. In 1960, two ancient gentlemen, Caspar Jr. and his brother Frank Borchard, stopped by our house near Paso Robles to share a noontime meal and to see the farm where we had moved after we left Newbury Park. After lunch, Caspar lifted up the tablecloth to examine the long, battle-scarred table that he and his wife Ida had given my parents years earlier. Caspar pointed to a wedge in the wood about the size of a boy's penknife. My mother hated the flaw and always covered it with a cloth when she had company. Caspar and Frank laughed and recalled the day they were roughhousing and one of them knocked the piece out. Their mother had boxed their ears and sent them off without dinner. For as long as she owned the table, their mother had covered the wedge. When her son Caspar Jr. and his wife needed a table for their growing family, she gave it to him because he had ruined it.

From that day on my mother left off the tablecloth. The wedge, like the old men who told the story, became a proud part of her heritage. One day a family member will inherit that table. Maybe it will go to my brother, Matt. Whoever gets it will recall a mother in 1888 and her young boys, roughhousing. More than a century later we remain connected.

As our brother Matt grew into adolescence he bore a striking resemblance to Tracy's twin. My brother carries family genes that render him dark and tall, serious and slow talking, just like Tracy's brother. When Matt's twin boys were born, fraternal like Uncle John and Tracy, we understood that their genes are alive and well in my brother's line.

CHAPTER FIFTEEN

A Thousand Oaks

THE SUBDIVISION OF Thousand Oaks from its inception attracted a strange assortment of investors. Many farmers viewed their new neighbors as misfits with dubious pasts and secrets to hide. Lou Long lived in an old ambulance. Others were circus people drawn by the employment opportunities of the Lion Farm. For the first few years the Conejo buzzed with rumors about its more colorful citizens, those who fled bad debts, investments gone awry with someone else's money or the law.

Thousand Oaks began modestly, with little more than a market, the Redwood Lodge, Jockey Meads, the Lion Farm, the Rock House, a gas station, three bars, Reverend Elver's Community Church and the grammar school. In the '30s, children bought penny candy from Nickel Brown, an old man who sold ice cream and candy through a little pass-through window in the front of his house.

In 1906, Henry Crowley inherited land in the area from his father. He purchased his brother's and sister's portions of the inheritance, but little happened. It was his son Frank, born in Newbury Park, who sold two large blocks of the farm in 1922, for housing developments. One was developed as Greenwich Village and the other sold to development partners Culver and Sturges.

John Kelley Sr. was leasing land from Frank Crowley and had it planted to barley when the sale to Culver and Sturges was finalized. The land was offered for sale to lot-hungry Los Angelenos with the proviso that the owners could not take possession until John's grain crop was harvested. A frenzy of land fever ensued. Culver and Sturges offered busses or touring cars that ran prospective buyers from Los Angeles. The developers' wives served lunch in their houses for the out-of-town speculators.

Excitement attracted both lookers and buyers who trudged into the ripening grain fields to mark their lots. Throughout the summer, the new owners returned in their own vehicles on Sundays to plant grapevines and rosebushes in the middle of the barley. John and Babe could do little more than watch. Finally it was time for John to harvest his crop. Although he exercised such care as he felt the situation required, nearly all of the vines and roses were destroyed when the crop was cut. He seemed unable to control his horses and they overpowered him, taking the rows right down the middle of the vines. In later years, whenever he told the story, his eyes twinkled with regret over the ruination of the bushes.

Eventually he purchased a house from E.B. Parks on Oak View Drive, in the heart of "Old Town." He and Babe lived there until they built a home on his land on Borchard Road near his mother, brothers and sisters.

From left: Fred, Walter & John Kelley, two cousins, Charlie Kelley, 1916.

As the town began to grow, it needed a name. Developers offered a prize of five dollars and a small lot for the best name. The winner was a young boy named Bobby Harrington, who attended Conejo School. The town was to be called *Thousand Oaks*.

In the 1940s, Fred Kelley Jr. and some of his teenage buddies decided to count the trees. They began in the center of town and worked outward until they had satisfied their curiosity. Fred has forgotten the actual number, but they found at least 1,000—more than enough to justify the town's claim. Some old-timers contend that at the time there were probably 20,000 oaks dotting the Conejo Valley.

Before Thousand Oaks existed, the Grande Union Hotel in Newbury Park provided a stopover for travelers dating back to 1876. It was constructed of redwood shipped from northern California lumber mills to Hueneme Wharf then freighted over the Potrero Grade in double wagons pulled by teams of eight draft horses. Early citizens traveled to Oxnard when they needed to be married, buried, attend high school or obtain groceries supplies at Simon Cohn's store. The Prussian Jewish merchant was the only store that extended credit to poor farmers. It was a long day's journey in a farm wagon. People of the Conejo didn't see an automobile until 1910.

Thousand Oaks was conceived in a burst of rugged individualism. For the first years, people with limited resources lived in makeshift tents while they constructed their houses. Farmers in the valley ignored the commotion as best they could. The development going on around them did not affect their routine; they had little use for the Lion Farm or their new neighbors. They stayed home and farmed.

From left: Irene Espinosa, Theresa Kelley, Rose Kelley 1914.

Newbury Park was older and more established than its upstart neighbor to the south. Ventura Boulevard was a dirt track to Los Angeles dotted with occasional farmhouses. At the time only a few homes and stores lay wedged to the south, near the school and hotel beyond the Borchard lands on the south and the Freidrich land on the north.

Ventu Park was a budding real estate development. The 500-acre development was divided into 4,000 lots, some so small that they were unbuildable. On the map the lots penciled out in tidy squares that ignored the hilly terrain and brushy eroded gullies. The square lots were large enough for only a small shack, but they were snapped up by movie stars who wanted a rustic hideaway, adventurous types who could do without the trappings of luxury, people who needed a cheap place to build, or homosexuals and others seeking a discreet place for a dalliance.

During the 1940s, one of the male members of the New York City Rothschilds built a big house near Moorpark Road and lived in relative seclusion while the town speculated about his reasons for being there. His lack of employment suggested that his family fortune supported his lifestyle. The CEO of Midstate Bank recalled that he earned his first paycheck hoeing weeds for Mr. Rothschild as a boy.

Ventu Park served as low-income housing during the Depression and the War years, until need for post-war housing required that lots be combined to allow larger houses. With suitable permanent housing available, the Conejo Valley began to grow. Ironically, today Newbury Park is noted in *Money* magazine as having the 4th highest median income in the country.

Newbury Park was never incorporated as a city. It was left to the mercy of county officials who seemed to take little interest in it even as the rest of the county developed. During the 1950s, rumors persisted of a feud between a County official and the would-be developer. Reba Hays Jeffries, granddaughter of Cecil Haigh, former owner of the Stagecoach Inn, worked tirelessly to keep Newbury Park from folding into the expanding influence of Thousand Oaks. When her efforts to incorporate failed, the town lay entangled in legal limbo for decades while neighboring Thousand Oaks exploded.

Thousand Oaks was without a high school until 1962. Camarillo High School opened in 1956. Before, students made a choice between attending school in Oxnard or Moorpark. Mr. Loyd Smith, whom everyone called "Smitty," drove the bus to Moorpark and after the return trip, parked the bus overnight next to his house in Thousand Oaks. Some years the route was 50 miles one way from Thousand Oaks to Santa Rosa Valley and into Moorpark. It was a long ride that began for some students before sunup. Another bus went through Camarillo, Camarillo Heights, Balcom Canyon and Moorpark. Following construction of Camarillo High School, the route was discontinued.

In the early days, recreation was home-grown. On the Hunt Ranch, a steep canyon, *salto* (Spanish for "jumping off place") featured a creek with a waterhole. The *Salto* reigned as the summer meeting place for young and old alike. Locals accessed it by a road through the Janss Ranch or by way of the Hunt Ranch Road. Men fished for trout, women brought picnic lunches and cooled watermelon in the running water. Children spent hot summer afternoons jumping from rope swings into the swimming hole. One mother noted in her journal how the swimming hole and the ranch creeks made life easier for her because she didn't have to bathe her children all summer. At the time, the water table was higher and even smaller creeks ran year-around.

Seminole Hot Springs, near Agoura, was developed as a trendy spa. Its sulfur water spewed from the earth from a pipe into a man-made swimming pool to soothe sore muscles and arthritic joints. Wealthy Jewish urbanites and movie people from Los Angeles flocked to the Hot Springs on weekends to see and be seen. Those who could not afford their own swimsuits rented the spa's black wool suits. Tracy, and later, my mother, recalled the ugly, scratchy swimming suits they wore while there. Eventually, Public Health laws required changes that the Hot Springs deemed financially unreasonable and the bathhouse went the way of progress.

Agoura and Calabasas remained a stretch of badland long after the disappearance of the highwaymen that had worried Rosa Kelley on her trek back to the Conejo in 1901. In the early days, the trip to Los Angeles was broken only by the Nine-Mile Café and the Triunfo Store. Later, Wonies Café at Brents Junction served as an oasis on the journey between Conejo and Hollywood. Before the advent of the automobile, trips were not taken lightly. The road was a dusty dirt ribbon that wound through bone-dry hills and valleys. Even before the Colorado River and Owens Valley water turned Los Angeles into a land of hybrid trees and patented roses, farmers of the nineteenth century had good reason to eschew the area in favor of the fertile farmlands to the northwest.

Chatsworth was sheep country. Mr. Poyer ran sheep on his ranch with the help of an old cowboy named Doc Dinsmore, whose wife taught school near Moorpark. Each year the arid land supported thousands of sheep. Even today, in towns with paper pretty names like Mission Viejo, broken adobe circles mark the abandoned ruins of holding pens where sheep once grazed.

The Russell Ranch, which never saw a sheep on its acreage, was sold to the Hearsts and eventually developed as Westlake Village. Depending on whose opinion one holds, the Westlake development marked the salvation or the death knell for the Conejo farmer.

Once it began, development happened quickly. Prior to 1922, a few large ranches and farms dominated the Valley. By the 1940s, many began to be divided or sold. Other remained: the Janss Ranch with its horses and cattle; the Lang Ranch with its grain and cattle; the McCrea Ranch, cattle and grain; the Pederson Ranch, chickens, citrus and grain; the Hunt Ranch; the Borchard Ranches; the Freidrich Ranch; Belle Holloway and her dairy; the Russell Ranch. Some of the ranches were still owned by their original owners, but others changed hands in the Depression when banks overextended credit and called in promissory notes that ranchers were unable to repay. Joel McCrea purchased his ranch in 1933 from a bank, after the Coffee Family lost it.

Mansey and Belle Holloway ran a dairy farm with the help of a milker known as Big Pockets. Every morning several milkers woke at three o'clock in the morning and herded the cows to a milking shed. Afterward, they drove the cows with empty udders and bellies into downtown Thousand Oaks to graze along the streets, crossing between cars and between buildings in Old Town. At five o'clock in the evening, Big Pockets herded the cows back for milking before penning them up for the night. The system worked. People braked for the cows, pedestrians watched for steaming cowpies and the byways were kept clipped.

Eventually, refrigeration and pasteurization laws became stricter, Mansey died and traffic in the town increased. Bell Holloway sold her cows to Chase Dairy in Oxnard and began a profitable business hauling horses. It's unknown what became of Big Pockets.

In the late '50s, Belle could be seen around town, a short, plump woman dressed in men's Levis with wide, turned-up cuffs and worn-out cowboy boots. Practicality ruled in every line of her body. She drank and swore, but she hated cigarettes and never smoked. She went by the name of "Ma". A big-hearted woman of the West, she served as honorary mayor. She kept down-and-outers employed, headed up community spirited events and added her brand of hospitality to Thousand Oaks.

During the 1920s, a Negro man, Mr. Henderson, opened the Green Tree Inn next to where the Redwood Lodge was later built on Ventura Boulevard. A dignified man, Mr. Henderson had been butler to a wealthy man named Mr. Pealer. When the old man died, his daughter, Miss

Florence Pealer and Mr. Henderson came to the Conejo and started the inn with her money. Mr. Henderson was an excellent innkeeper and chef, widely traveled, and was quite sophisticated for the budding town. Miss Pealer added her artistic talents to creating ambiance in the popular inn.

For a few years during the Great Depression, Oscar Olsen worked at the Green Tree Inn, in the evenings or between farming seasons. Hired at first as a janitor and general handyman, he eventually waited tables, washed dishes and worked large parties and banquets. Some of the townspeople seemed unduly concerned with Oscar's business. He ignored them because he needed the money, but more than that, Mr. Henderson was having difficulty hiring help. Oscar endured some taunting and mild threats by citizens who thought he should stick to farming and stop associating with Negroes.

A number of Klu Klux Klansmen had moved into Thousand Oaks during the late 1920s. By 1929, their numbers were sufficient for them to muster support. Mr. Henderson became the target of a vocal minority who objected to a black businessman. They also noticed his white female associate, Miss Pealer.

Jean Olsen recalled the day two men drove to the farm and threatened to beat up her father and his family if he didn't "stop working for a colored man." Stubborn, determined to support his family and abide by his principles, Oscar refused to quit. The family grew wary of strangers coming to the farm. They did most of their trading in Moorpark and avoided Thousand Oaks except when Oscar worked a shift.

Late in 1929, the KKK circulated a rumor that Mr. Henderson and Miss Pealer's relationship was more than a business arrangement. In a flurry of anti-black sentiment, Henderson was driven out of the Inn. He had leased the property from a local land company and the payment was paid ahead, but the lender bowed to public pressure and cancelled the lease without citing a reason. With no place to live, Henderson and Miss Peale retrieved as many personal possessions as they could and set up housekeeping on a plot of land behind the Olsen's apricot orchard with another woman, Miss Nielson.

Oscar built a house out of two one-room bungalows that they salvaged from their Green Tree Auto Court, a row of rental units behind the Inn that they owned. He and Henderson waited for a dark night when the town was asleep, and slid the bungalows onto skids. He used his automobile to drag the buildings from Thousand Oaks along Moorpark Road.

Miss Pealer draped the walls with genuine Navajo Indian blankets for insulation. She and her friend Miss Nielson filled the rooms with artistic sculptures of her own creation. Miss Pealer sometimes served tea and showed my mother treasures from her travels.

When the atmosphere eased, Henderson accepted a position as a butler for a wealthy family in Lake Sherwood. Miss Pealer engaged an architect who built a lovely home on the west side of the highway, far up on a hillside near the Russell Ranch. By the end of the year the stock market crashed and the racist citizens of Thousand Oaks had worse problems to worry about. Miss Pealer continued to live in her hillside mansion until her death.

———————

Coincidence twists and turns like ribbon throughout the history of the Conejo, linking the past to the present, one person to another. Memories were long, but so were friendships. In the late 1940s, Oscar's oldest daughter Arthelia took a job at American Commercial and Savings Bank in Moorpark, working for a branch manager named Aloyisis Honerkamp.

In 1950, a young Mexican man, Mike Loza, came to see Mr. Honerkamp about borrowing five hundred dollars. He owned a thriving bar in Moorpark and served tacos and Mexican food as bar food. It was his dream to start a Mexican restaurant. He rented a little house in Camarillo, expanded his restaurant until he outgrew the space. He wanted to build a real restaurant and felt he could make a go of it, but he had applied to several banks and had been turned down. Mr. Honerkamp sized up the young man and gave him the loan.

A few years passed. After the end of WW II, Arthelia married the banker's son, "Jack" Honerkamp. Mr. Loza outgrew his little restaurant in Moorpark, named simply, *Mike Loza's*, and built a larger one on Lewis Road in Camarillo with a bank loan from Mr. Honerkamp Sr. *El Tecolote* became a landmark. For the rest of his life, Mr. Loza would not accept payment from Jack whenever the family stopped for a meal on their way through the area.

Eventually the elder Mr. Honerkamp retired from American Commercial and Savings and began a second career with Bank of America. For several years he visited Timber and Conejo schools every Thursday for "Bank Day." He provided each student with a savings passbook and a sturdy cardboard savings envelope with a red string fastener that twisted around two cardboard buttons. Very official. On

Wednesdays, teacher reminded their students to bring their envelopes with at least 25 cents inside. The next day he carried deposits to the Bank of America in Camarillo. On his way home he dropped the empty envelopes at the school office with each deposit noted in our savings passbook.

No matter how poor we were, we found three quarters, one for my sister, brother and me. Making a regular deposit became a point of pride. Mr. Honerkamp was our cousins' grandfather and we felt honor-bound to make a good showing. I overheard my mother and Arthelia talking one day. The bank had put Grandpa Allie on notice; he would lose his job if Bank Day deposits didn't pick up. I added the money I earned picking blackberries at my parent's roadside stand and managed to save $132.26 by the time the program ended in 1958.

CHAPTER SIXTEEN

Lighter Times

THE MOVIE INDUSTRY brought money into the valley at a time when farm prices were falling. During the Depression years, farmers sat on their acreage and tried to make a living. Farmland in the Conejo was as cheap as anywhere else. Ours was not a family that aspired to go into commerce. Before the land had development value, we had no choice but to farm.

Some people tried making a fast buck, but word spread quickly in a small community. For a brief period in the mid-1930s, four men ran a grocery store near Thousand Oaks with exceptional prices. Fred Kelley Sr. and his family counted themselves fortunate to be savvy customers who patronized their store. In 1938, the men's photographs appeared on the front page of the *Times*. They had been arrested in Oxnard, in possession of four trucks filled with stolen groceries from Safeway, A&P Market and two smaller grocery stores. With some embarrassment, Fred moved his trade back to another grocery store.

After Will Rogers advised actor Joel McCrea to invest in land in the Conejo, other movie stars followed. Suddenly plain farmers and the famous lived side-by-side. Joel McCrea's ranch headquarters sat behind whitewashed outbuildings at the base of the Norwegian Grade. He and Nick Olsen were neighbors; their ranches butted up against each other at the top of the Grade. No one called him "Joel." Neither was he "Mr. McCrea." In the neighborhood everyone called him "Joel McCrea." Joel McCrea was a regular neighbor. He sent his children to school with poor farmers' children, but he augmented their education by paying for class trips to Los Angeles museums. He provided ice cream sodas and banana splits for his sons' classmates. Whenever his latest movie came out, he arranged for classes to take a field trip to the Moorpark movie house to see a special showing.

Across Oscar's fence on the neighboring Janss Ranch, a false-front western town was built as a movie set. It was a make-believe town with tarps covering one wall of each room to allow camera access. From Tracy's front porch we could watch stagehands roll paper-mache boulders from a horse-drawn hay wagon. Within minutes the workers converted bare hillsides into rocky bluffs and canyons. Mounted extras would spend long stretches sitting on their horses, smoking cigarettes and talking while the scene was being set up. When the cameras rolled, we watched riders run pell-mell down the canyon, hotly pursued by the Indians they had been visiting with only minutes before. In my innocence the mystery was ruined. Cowboys weren't supposed to like the Indians.

My brother Mel was more adventurous. He crept to the top of the bluffs and lay on a cliff watching filming of a western movie. He went back to Grandpa's house and told his aunt and uncle, Mary and Neil. They wanted to see so he took them back to watch, but the filming was over for the day. No one was around so they walked down a gap in the rimrock and found remnants left from the shoot. Paper mache boulders, large and small as if more rocks were needed. He found a real wooden arrow with a rubber arrowhead and a car axel shaft used for staking down the rocks, which he lugged all the way home. High adventure for a 12-year-old.

The dynamics of the set were easy to define. Cowboys wore white hats; Bad men wore black. The movie Indians were invariably the bad guys, with bloodcurdling yelps and flying rubber arrows. Movie-set Indians wore lots of feathers and war paint, and looked suspiciously like Caucasians with bad wigs and greasy makeup. Filming lasted only a minute or two before the "cut" command was given and they would gather in a clump of horses to laugh and light fresh cigarettes. Across the fence we could watch the action, but the sounds were lost in the wind.

Television was still new to us in the mid '50s; we didn't know about suspended disbelief. We didn't want to know that nothing was real, nothing was permanent. Looking back, the plots and action, the fake backdrops and sound effects were so amateurish that years later, we laughed at our naiveté. But as kids we were captivated. Ironically, those early westerns were rife with authentic saddles and gear, worn clothing and hats, scruffy extras who rode horses like they'd grown up on one. No consultants were needed; script writers and stage managers had lived the authentic western life.

In the early westerns, action was the thing. To say that plot suffered was an understatement. The camera captured long views of chases with a generous dose of raw action and scenery. Punches swung in silence with the crisp "pow!" dubbed in at the studio. The whinny of horses, the creak of leather, even the cattle trucks off-loading livestock in the morning gave us a sense of being part of the action. But, alas, an era ended. Far sooner than we were ready to let them go, Oscar moved from the Conejo and we no longer had a front row seat to the action. For the rest of our days we watched the background of every TV western to see if we recognized the location.

Janss Road was dirt until the ranch was developed in the 1950s. Some confusion existed about the spelling of their name. Early newspapers reported the name as "Janns," as often as "Janss." Sometimes reporters spelled it "Jans." The Janss family hired local men to cowboy their cattle, hoe their lima beans and farm their dry land. Many of us didn't realize the extent of the family holdings. To us they were merely farmers and ranchers like the rest of the Conejo. Their family house set up a long driveway, hidden from Highway 101 by a row of bushes. The Janss kids attended Timber School with us, with little fanfare.

My cousin, John Kelley III (Nonnie), was a friend of the Janss boys the year Disneyland opened in 1955. He was in third grade when the father flew them to Anaheim in his private plane. On Monday, my brother and I pumped our cousin for details, but he seemed at a loss about where to start. He told us they had jumped up and down on the beds, having a pillow fight until a down pillow split open and feathers covered the room. Mr. Janss called room service and the maids moved them into another room for the night.

One morning in the mid-fifties, dogs along Borchard Road woke us with their wild barking. Soon we heard the sounds of syncopated drumming and shouting. As my sisters and I watched from the bend in the road, a caravan of camels and elephants paraded past our house. For a week, the air reverberated with strange bellowing in the canyon behind Borchard Road. The telephone tree started up and we heard that Cecil de Mille was doing a shoot in the hills behind Newbury Park for a biblical movie with a cast of thousands. The scuttlebutt declared it was a scene for *The Ten Commandments*.

In my mother's childhood, a circus train offloaded each year at the depot in Moorpark. Trainers marched their elephants single-file along Moorpark Road, up the Norwegian grade to the Lion Farm. The caravan traveled at night when the traffic was light. A man holding a lantern rode on the front elephant while another man, similarly equipped, rode the last elephant. The caravan snaked across the darkness with two tiny beacons bobbing a warning for automobiles. At the end of the circus run the caravan would reverse the journey—two opportunities for the Olsens to drive to the end of their road, cut their auto lights and watch. Nothing seemed impossible in those days. No permits were required. In the absence of laws prohibiting it, anything was allowed. If a caravan of elephants or a herd of sheep or cattle happened to be passing, the prudent motorist simply pulled over and waited.

In 1938, a movie location scout stopped by Oscar's farm to discuss staging a movie on the rugged bluffs overlooking his pasture. The scout wanted to rent the location and the sheep he saw grazing nearby. Oscar would need to agree, as would his brother Nick and Rich Pederson. The Samuel Goldwyn, Inc. Ltd. Legal Department drew up contracts for all three to sign—Oscar's for rental of the farmland, entrance rights, sheep and straw.

A crew arrived in early spring to dig holes into the bluff which they filled with clay pots of blooming heather. Overnight a hundred yards of craggy bluff became the Scottish Highlands. Crews built a narrow gauge track up the backside of the bluff, out of camera range. They fitted a cart onto it that would take the actors and supplies up the hill, pulled by men and a rope at the top. Later, Merle Oberon was afraid to ride in the cart to the top of the hill so two men were assigned the job of carrying her up and down the hill. Prop men laid false fences across the flats. When the heather scenes were completed, crews sprinkled the cliffs with asbestos snow.

Jean Olsen, 12 at the time, earned $5 a day to herd her father's 85 sheep. She was hired to dress as a scruffy little boy and herd the sheep. For three days she was allowed to miss school—in her opinion even better than taking her meals in the catering line alongside stars whose faces she didn't recognize: Merle Oberon, Lawrence Olivier and David Niven. At the time she had never attended a picture show. She thought the pretty lady in the food line was the Queen.

Oscar earned $200 for the use of his pastures. The fences and lumber from the props were left behind for his and Nick's use. The sheep earned $2.50 each. Presumably he and Tracy used the money for their herd's benefit. When *Wuthering Heights* was released, Oscar was not sufficiently impressed to take his family to see it at the theater in Moorpark.

Other movies were made in the Norwegian Colony, including *How Green Is My Valley, Spartacus* and several of the Lassie movies, including *Lassie Come Home.*

Life in the 1950s was idyllic for a kid growing up amid an extended family network. One of the relatives mentioned to my father that the Lion Farm needed oat hay. I rode along on a couple of summer afternoons when we delivered it down a narrow alley in Thousand Oaks, me dodging an elephant trunk that was trying to grab my blonde hair, and later, suffering camel slime when it spit on me as I tried frantically to roll up the window.

Once the Lion Farm changed names, posters and billboards sprung up for the new, improved *Jungleland.* Locals may have flocked there on a regular basis, but I only attended once, in 1957, with my cousin Jill Ashby. Her teenaged brother Juney drove us from Newbury Park in his new Isetta with the radio blaring "That'll be the Day" by Buddy Holly. He reluctantly handed us the only bill in his wallet, a $20, with a stern warning to bring back the change. Our answer was lost as he floored his gas pedal and spun off in a hail of gravel, his *Butch Wax* pomaded ducktail unfazed by the wind.

Jill was upset with her brother that day. She intended to spend Juney's money and she co-opted me into helping by assuring me he wouldn't care. The entrance fee was $1.25. Sodas were a quarter, certainly more than the ones in the grocery store. We had a soda along with a hamburger and fries. We shopped the gift store. Coming from a large family, I wasn't familiar with the concept of retail therapy, but I settled on some pretty ceramic zebras and a miniature dinosaur, which I offered to return to Juney when he finished shouting at us on the way home.

By the time we were ready to be picked up, we had run out of ideas for spending the last six dollars. We offered it to Mable Stark and her 18 ferocious Sumatran tigers, but she declined. Jill gave a generous tip to the glamorous elephant trainer's assistant. We were fascinated with the way the elephant wrapped its trunk around her scantily-clad body while she whirled and dipped, all the time maintaining a confident smile. Eleven and 10 years old respectively, Jill and I saw womanhood in her heavy mascara, short pink leotard that revealed her considerable charms, fishnet stockings and gold ballet shoes. Our tip was *homage* paid to glamour and, although I couldn't put a name to it at the time, to sex appeal.

We still had $4 and change left when Juney picked us up. He yelled at us all the way home. Still, it was the best day of my life. Undoubtedly, Silas Kelley would have approved of his granddaughters enjoying themselves on such a grand scale. Caspar Borchard Sr. would have been appalled.

The hills that briefly bloomed with Samuel Goldwyn's heather were home to rattlesnakes that had been multiplying since Indian times. When Oscar and his neighbors bladed ground to build his barn, eighteen rattlers slithered from a hole the tractor opened in the bank. Oscar used dynamite, the farmer's go-to for troublesome rodents and tree trunks. Rattlesnakes were a farmer's nemesis, notorious for striking the faces and legs of sheep and horses—and small children if they didn't stay alert. In the era before environmentalism, making a living meant taming the land. Farming took precedence over the vagaries of nature. Oscar subscribed to the Audubon Society magazine, but he protected his crops and livestock with a vengeance.

When he was 10, Neil Olsen used his new B.B. gun to shoot blackbirds out of trees. He thought he would impress his classmates by telling them of his successful shots, despite the fact that he was president of the Audubon Club that year. He didn't make a distinction between the two deeds until his teacher pointed out his hypocrisy. His classmates were so upset that they impeached him.

An ancient Indian cave overlooked the farm on the north edge of Oscar's land. The overhang was painted with petroglyphs in red and black; arrows and frogs, and strange markings that had held their secrets through the ages. Jean Olsen spoke of seeing unbroken stone bowls and grinding stones, arrowheads and beads. We were allowed to visit the caves, but not to touch. In later years the caves were desecrated, but for the years that Norwegians owned the property, the cave remained a sacred spot.

To stand on the bluffs in the evening with my grandfather as we searched for lost sheep, when the setting sun reached its last fingers across the golden grass, was a proud and timeless moment. The winds churned the grass in the narrows and sang in the hills in a way that made the cliffs seem alive. A century after Nils Olsen embraced the land, native grasses still dropped seeds to the earth before the rains. Without sheep to keep them cropped, the hillside soon abounded in cactus fields. Too steep for a tractor, the hills have held their identity through the ages.

The remoteness of the farm was a problem for Jean and her sister Arthelia when they were girls growing up alone on Olsen Road. During their childhood they were not the best of friends. Camaraderie came later with shared motherhood. During the early years one girl was interested in the outdoors, the other remained content to learn domestic skills. One was Oscar's helper, the other, Tracy's. The division was clear and long-lasting.

During the Depression, farm families offered a safe haven for city families where both parents worked long hours to earn a living. Los Angeles provided cash paychecks to men who labored in the city while farmers were cash poor but with a full pantry. It was not unusual for the two factions to team up. Complete strangers boarded their children on farms and visited on weekends when they could afford the gasoline—sometimes not for months.

For several summers Tracy's cousin Irene sent her children Nelda and Betty to the farm. Irene's father was one of Silas Kelley's brothers. Irene's husband worked as a foreman at a lemon packing shed near Pasadena. When my mother spoke of her childhood years, Nelda and Betty figured so prominently into her stories that we felt as though we knew them, even though we'd never met. Mom took us to Los Angeles to visit Nelda when I was ten. Our mothers hoped their children could become friends like they had been, but we stood apace, overwhelmed with shyness.

A few years later two brothers, Frank and Howard, fostered at Tracy's house while their mother Mazzie operated a boat business out of Newport Beach. Their parents were divorced, the father worked as a scientist at the Griffith Park Observatory. They were five and seven, almost the same age as Tracy's young son, Neil—good company for him. They lived on the farm for two years until the father remarried.

A few years later Timmy came to stay for a year while his father worked in the Hollywood film industry.

Through similar circumstances we began a lifelong association with another family, and gained another aunt and three cousins in the bargain. Arthelia's best friend in third grade was a little girl named Melva. She lived with her grandparents, the Coffees, on a ranch at the bottom of the Norwegian Grade. During the Depression they lost the ranch and Joel McCrea bought it from the bank. Tracy and Melva's mother Boe became friends. Boe was Protestant, artistic, divorced, fashion-conscious and chic. Tracy was Catholic, grounded and practical. They seemed to have nothing in common, but they supported each other with their strengths. One had roots, the other had wings.

After a few years, Boe remarried and moved away with her new husband. Through the years she and her daughter returned to visit, sometimes coming to spend several weeks at the farm when the husband was searching for work in the city. The Depression was hard on artistic people. When the husband was employed, Boe's home life sparkled with exotic ambiance. The family acquired a spider monkey, a turtle, pheasants and a goat, most of which eventually ended up on the Olsen Farm when they moved.

Mary Olsen spent two weeks with Boe in a remote cabin in a canyon near Pasadena, while Boe wrote children's stories and sent them off to national magazines for publication. Mary accompanied her in the hope that the climate would help her asthma. She recalls driving to the drop-off point at the base of the canyon and loading their provisions onto a burro, a process that took several hours. It was late afternoon by the time they set off along a narrow path along a creek. The burro picked its way in the gathering gloom and arrived at the cabin's front door in total darkness. During the entire two weeks, Mary recalls seeing no visitors.

When Boe's husband was off on jobs as an electrician, she and her daughter lived for three years in a small rental on Oscar's property. Melva attended high school in Moorpark while Boe sold Raleigh products from her old Austin automobile. Tracy rode with her once and had her purse stolen, along with her precious lifetime driver's license. The customer helped them look for the missing purse, but it was not to be found. Tracy thought the woman had slipped it under a sofa blanket and hid it. Later after Boe and her husband separated and reconciled and moved to the Rock House in Thousand Oaks. He was killed when a train struck his car.

Boe sewed with more ambition than skill. She had mastered only the basic rudiments of sewing, but she created her wardrobe with a designer's flare. Most of her clothing came from Los Angeles thrift stores: old coats and dresses that she tore apart for the fabric. A black and white polka-dot skirt became an elegant scarf right off the pages of *Vogue* magazine.

In her later years, she lost an eye to brain cancer and wore a neat white eye bandage beneath her eyeglasses. She wound her hair into an exquisite, snowy-white coil held together with combs and long hairpins. To me she was glamour personified.

Tracy opened her home and her heart to her city friends. What she received must have been a fair trade because she and Boe struck a friendship that has flourished through four generations.

Melva grew up and married a tall, elegant man named Frederick. Her babies arrived in years when my aunt's didn't, so they traded baby clothes back and forth. Her husband became an executive at RCA Records. He was the first man we ever knew who wore a suit to work. He was also a Christian Science practitioner, as elusive a concept to us as Aimee Semple McPhearson had been to the Olsens when they saw the woman preaching in a revival tent on Charles Street, in Moorpark in the late 1920s. He worked at the RCA building in Hollywood. We were unsure about his position, but he had shaken hands with Elvis in 1959, so he was pretty "high up." Hadn't his father been a concert pianist who spent years teaching voice and elocution to the silent screen stars when "talkies" came in? Frederick supplied Roman candles and fireworks for our Fourth of July celebrations, fireworks that he picked up during trips to Mexico.

Holidays created a host of lifetime memories. Easter was the big one. In the early years, when Oscar was still on his Conejo farm, he hosted what everyone called, "Oscar's picnic" —even though Tracy did most of the work. It was always held at "Tracy's house," always outdoors, sometimes under the patio cover after we thrashed the flowerbeds for rattlesnakes and covered the tables with checkered tablecloths. Sometimes we picnicked on the *Wuthering Heights* bluffs where we could see the entire Norwegian Colony. The celebration included Nick and his family, and a host of regulars whose relationship I never fully understood. Most were Tracy's cousins of some sort.

Fathers and children flew kites on the bluffs while mothers chatted and laid out the picnic. If rains had brought spring grass, we took turns sliding down the slick slopes on sheets of flattened tin, the same slopes that Oscar's father had showed him as a boy. We ran up and down the earthen steps the *Wuthering Heights* crew had dug when they built a rail cart track for their equipment two decades earlier. We hunted Easter eggs in the pastures or in the lawns and bushes around the house.

Later, we picked oranges and lemons in season to take home. One couple always filled five-gallon jugs with water from the well because they believed the water was purer. Before the party broke up, Oscar invariably brought out his Brownie camera and took a group photo with black and white film.

Sometimes Rich Pederson attended, and possibly his brothers, but their relationship with the Olsens seemed less about shared family than shared land. The two families may have experienced the usual rifts and disagreements over the years as happens when men see things differently, but they were lifetime neighbors and Oscar always spoke well of them.

Summer vacations were spent at a beach cabin at Hollywood-by-the-Sea in Oxnard. The development began in the 1940s with high aspirations that included laid out streets, city water and cement sidewalks until WW II quelled the plans. In the '40s, Tracy spent $250 of her inheritance on a 20x70-foot lot. The lot was one of the first sold and its location was ideal. The Pacific Ocean lay across the street, a quick walk over hot sand for little feet—to waves breaking in slow rolls and shimmering to foam on the gradually sloping sand shelf. The sand was white and crystalline, deep enough that as children with shovels and buckets, we thought we could dig to China.

In the years shortly after WW II, Oscar pitched a huge army surplus tent that covered most of the lot. For years, summer and winter, the tent stood as a permanent fixture. When my mother was a teenager, Tracy placed dressers inside and stored swimsuits and clothing in the drawers. The tent stored cooking gear, pots and pans, lanterns and chairs. Oscar set a cast iron cook stove in the sand. On each visit he dug a hole down to water level where the sand was damp and cool. In this hollow he placed a wooden box that served as a food cooler.

Until they purchased their own lot, Tracy's brother John and Babe parked their travel trailer on the lot and some of the children were allowed to sleep in it. No one ever broke in or stole anything.

In the mid-1940s, the tent began to rot. At the same time, grandchildren began to come along. Oscar constructed a one-room cabin with clapboard siding and a tiny bathroom with a sheet metal shower stall, a stove and a kitchen sink with running water. A raised alcove held a double bed, sectioned off with a curtain. A hideaway bed served two lucky children, usually my cousin Helen and me, since we were the oldest girls. In those days seniority settled most disputes. He fenced the lot to keep in toddlers.

Down a long block at the end of Pacific Street, a chain link concertina fence separated civilians from the deep water channel leading to Port Hueneme. Once each summer a low, bellowing horn signaled the departure of the battleship U.S.S. Norton Sound on its way to sea duty. We children would race down the sidewalk and cluster against the fence to wave at the sailors standing at attention on the deck. Once, my father stood beside me as we watched the battleship churn the waters. He snapped to attention and saluted the sailors. After a moment he recalled himself and glanced over, half-embarrassed. Tears glistened in his eyes and I knew he was recalling his own Navy days a decade earlier. The moment ended and we turned back toward the beach cabin as the ship's horn sounded long into the distance. The next year when the battleship passed, I imagined my father in his dress blues, standing on deck while the wind whipped his kerchief.

We visited the beach cabin as often as our mothers would take us. Sometimes Melva and her brood came, too. It was a process to gather enough clothes, food and diapers for growing families. A trip to the beach was seldom a one-day event. Poor roads and old cars made for slow travel, and then there was the task of getting everyone sanded off and into the car for the ride home. If we went, we stayed for at least a three-day weekend. But a full week was even better.

Tracy shared the double bed with my mother or my aunt, depending on who was pregnant at the time. Oscar slept outside with the men and children, under canvas tarps fastened to the fence. If fog threatened, he pitched a tent or a lean-to, but by the mid-'50s it had to be disassembled at the end of each visit to protect against theft and vandalism.

Each morning our mothers smeared our exposed skin with whatever was on sale at the market—usually baby oil or zinc oxide—and sent us out to play in the shady side of the fenced sandlot. When our cheeks burned we remembered to wear our hats and long sleeve shirts. When any one of us became cranky, we all had to take naps under a cluster of striped beach umbrellas that shaded a 20-foot square section of the beach. Coppertone sunscreen was new on the market, at a price prohibitive for mothers with a lot of arms and legs to cover. By the first day our fair skin would be pink. By the end of the week we were peeling.

The vacation ended when the mothers' nerves were frayed and Tracy's generosity destroyed by 11 children under the age of 12, sunburned, cranky from lack of sleep, over- stimulation and too much sugar. What a wonderful week!

The first weekend in September marked the end of summer. Every year we celebrated with a huge family barbecue, a birthday cake and hand-churned ice cream. In addition to it being my birthday, it was Labor Day weekend and the opening of dove season. Our family of farmers and hunters, city men and adopted cousins took to the fields while the women made plans for Thanksgiving and Christmas. As a kid, I assumed that everyone came together to celebrate my birthday—after all, everyone brought presents and sang "Happy Birthday." One year when I was 14, I was sent to call the men for dinner and candle blowing. No one wanted to leave their hunting blinds. I explained that it was time to cut my cake.

No interest. On the long, lonely walk back to the farmhouse, I realized that our family reunion had never been about my birthday. Instead of being favored among the clan, I was merely a child with a luck birth-date. It was truly a shock to me.

Christmas didn't just happen. It was coordinated in long phone conversations and letters between Tracy, my mother and the aunts. By Christmas vacation cousins began to arrive. Some years we waited to roll out the sugar cookies until we were all together. Tracy would have the cookie dough ready. She would pull out huge bowls of chilled, almond-flavored and gingerbread dough, pull off the waxed paper and set everything in the middle of her vast table. We'd roll out dough and press cutters while she slid pans into the oven. Our tools of trade were child-sized rolling pins that Oscar had turned on his lathe from seasoned apricot limbs, and child-sized aprons that Tracy sewed from gingham. Memories of cookies baking, fireplace crackling, carols playing in the living room, stern voices fussing when flour dusted the floor, pans of cookies in a dozen different shapes, cookie cutters she'd collected over a lifetime, homemade colored sugar—red and green—and if we were lucky, one container of store-bought sprinkles to share. And afterward, aluminum push-tubes of homemade frosting.

We cousins enjoyed each other. We loved and respected each other's parents because they were as likely to call us on our stuff as our own. One year, a couple who had sat near us at a beach trip remarked as they were leaving that they'd spent the day trying to figure out which kid belonged to which mother. My mother and her sisters took it as a compliment.

In photographs taken at our childhood birthday parties we can name each guest—even fifty years later. Everyone is a cousin.

Some cousins recall only criticism from Tracy. They failed to forge a bond, a failing that was not their fault. As firstborn granddaughter I have no explanation except that she was old when the last babies were born. Her energy had been diffused by a lifetime of coping with problems. Over the years she grew fretful and short-tempered. She became occupied with health problems like arthritis that sapped her strength and good cheer. The tag-end grandchildren suffered. Some of the grandchildren came as a package when her youngest daughter Mary married a widower with five children. The step-grandchildren do not recall Tracy with the fondness I do, but they enjoyed the same bond with their father's mother, who helped rear them after their mother died.

Some of them thought she was cranky, but the truth may be more benign. Tracy possessed a relaxed, benevolent nature that she indulged on a one-to-one basis. Task oriented, she looked to grandchildren to do their fair and proper share—much less than she had done at their age. When faced with an overload of grandchildren, she saw only the meals that needed to be cooked and the beds that needed to be made. There was never time for her to relax, to take them shopping or to get to know them as individuals.

When Oscar and Tracy took summer road trips, they invited their grandchildren along. Oscar kept a journal. His account of a trip he and Tracy took to the State Fair in 1940 contained a description of road conditions, farms and fruitstands, weather and picnics along the way. Of course the car was filled with children, in this case, a daughter and two nieces.

I was 11, the year I took my trip with them. There were five of us in their GMC pickup and camper bound for Vancouver. My brother and I rode in the camper shell. For two weeks we shared a motel room with grandparents and my then-unmarried aunt Mary. We dined together, fished and cooked our catch at river's edge. We watched Oscar admit to the Canadian Border inspector that we had fresh fruit in the car, and watched as the inspector tossed our succulent ripe peaches into a trash bin. Consequence was a hard master, but a lesson I never forgot.

Oscar taught us how to read a compass, to query about room rates and to inspect a motel room before renting it. We discussed current events and asked questions about the old days. We watched Oscar shave gray stubble from his aging chin and Tracy clean partial plates in a glass of fizzing water. We visited botanical gardens and learned to curb our impatience when we passed tourist spots more interesting to our ages. Following Oscar's example, we bought maps and logged our day's progress every evening. We jotted travel notes in our journals. Oscar showed us how to mark our travel map so we would remember where we'd been. We thrived by example.

Through the years they managed to include all their grandchildren in their road trips. As long as they were able, they traveled to Yellowstone and Zion, across Canada and the East Coast, and to the deserts of the Southwest. They took my mother and some of my siblings to Ohio to meet my father's parents while the rest of us stayed home to work the farm.

Traveling with grandparents at the brink of adolescence formed a lasting impression. We observed our grandparents as we were forming ideas about relationships. They gave us firsthand knowledge about growing older with grace and wisdom. They taught us to live frugally so that we could enjoy our retirement years. Visiting her deathbed, I remembered to tell Tracy "Thank you" one last time. Our trips with them are memories that bind us.

For my grandparents, travel was a luxury that arrived after Tracy began selling off her acres on Borchard Road. My mother and her siblings were reared in a leaner time when their father struggled with a variety of jobs to supplement the farm income. Oscar never made more than $300 a month in his life. Tracy never held a job outside the home. But among rural farmers, everyone lived about the same scale—give or take. If Oscar and Tracy lived better, in our minds, it was because they were industrious and frugal. In 1936, they purchased a new car and a farm truck because the old vehicles were held together with baling wire and wouldn't make it another mile. Depression prices for manufactured foods had hit rock bottom; it was a good time to buy. To afford the purchases, they put their daughters to work on the farm and cut out all the extras. They didn't replace the vehicles until after WW II.

Through 40 years of farming, Oscar and Tracy had their share of setbacks: drought, weather, crop failures and difficulty getting hired help. One year during the Depression, men drove into the apricot orchards and picked the trees clean while the family slept. An entire year's income disappeared overnight.

Oscar's cancelled bank checks, saved in a box for nearly 70 years, give clues to their circumstances. Each month he wrote only a half-dozen checks. In 1926, Tracy wrote one to the grocery store in Moorpark for $5.23 to pay off their monthly charge. By 1946, the monthly charge had increased to $15.78. When natural gas came to the Conejo, Oscar paid three dollars. On one occasion he paid the Borchard Brothers $15.00 to level a field for planting alfalfa. A few times a year Tracy ordered from Sears & Roebuck. Her checks, written for $19.50, were often the largest expenditures of the year.

Bank of A. Levy owned some of the biggest farms in the Conejo. In some cases farmers owed more than their land was worth, but bank officials deemed it in their best interests to allow the farmers to remain on the land rather than foreclosing. In time, escalating land values saved many a family from foreclosure.

Oscar never borrowed from a bank. In his younger days this inability to take out a loan caused friction between him and his father. While the

Pedersons borrowed to expand their citrus orchards and to purchase tractors and equipment, the Olsens maintained a strict cash policy.

The source of friction was a deep chasm between Nils Olsen and his sons. They might have taken a loan against their farms, but their father didn't trust banks. Nils kept his name on the deeds to his sons' lands and he refused to sign any bank loan papers. Seeing the Pedersons improve their land with bank loans didn't sway Nils's opinion. He had lived through the Depression and saw farmers stripped of their land. He had seen his friend Lina Hansen forced to sell her farm in order to pay probate taxes after her husband's death.

Oscar's 1906 Webster's Dictionary was worn and dog eared, the result of his need to learn a second language from its pages. He didn't learn to speak English until he started school. Such things are good to know about a grandfather. Many of us recall sitting beside Oscar as he tried to teach us to count to ten in Norwegian. Like many immigrants' children, he could not write his childhood language, he could only recall snatches from the spoken language of his memory. He tried to teach us. Over and over I would recite, *en, to, tre, fire, fem, seks, sju, åtte, ni, ti*. How hard my little brain struggled to retain the strange sounds, to be able to recite them the next time Oscar asked. But the task seemed impossible. My mother was no help. She hadn't learned her father's childhood language. Perhaps Oscar had become nostalgic in his later years and realized the value of retaining his culture. Perhaps he was too busy making a living to teach his own children. He would be pleased, I think, to know that some of his grandchildren still remember.

In time, Oscar and Nick outlived the pastoral ambiance of their valley. In 1955, Nick was selling a section of his land. They decided that the Olsen Cemetery would need to be moved. They got permission from Norway to move the Hanson family's remains along with their own and the Pedersons.

Oscar and Nick gathered on a crisp morning, along with Pete, Rich and Lawrence Pederson, to witness the disinterment of those buried there. The County Coroner oversaw the backhoe driver as he unearthed the broken bits of 14 wooden coffins, six of them child-sized. The children's remains were combined into a single metal casket and reinterred in the Ivy Lawn Memorial Park in Ventura. A stone monument with their names marks their resting place, Section F, Block

25, Lot 6. Oscar and Nick purchased a second casket for the hired men: Jorgen Ness, 31, shot with his own gun under questionable circumstances and Martin Peterson, 28, run over by a hay wagon—the last soul to be interred in the Olsen Cemetery.

The Olsen Cemetery in 1955, with fence removed for reinterment at Ivy Lawn Cemetery.

CHAPTER SEVENTEEN

Paying the Piper

IN 1957, A group of Italians from New Jersey moved their families into the Conejo and the valley began to change. They seemed wrapped in a shroud of mystery. Some of their children began attending Timber School. In the next years, 4,000 homes were built on the Janss Ranch. Some of the first houses were built so quickly and cheaply that weeds grew through cracks in the foundation. In others, porches and corners broke away from the rest of the house. Lawsuits couldn't be filed because the construction company disbanded and formed under another name before anything could be done. The county lacked building inspectors. These were topics that adults quietly discussed over coffee. Farmers worried that their own land might attract unwanted attention from developers. All of this helped to fuel the drive to leave the Conejo. Years later, the newspaper's explanation of Mr. Janss's fall from a hotel room in Los Angeles never rang true for some of the farmers who learned about it.

Around the same time, Mr. Sarto, an old man who owned a bakery in the San Fernando Valley, began calling on Walter Kelley. On Sunday mornings he arrived with pastries and kitchen table conversation about the world outside the Conejo. Walter began to look forward to his visits. The baker wanted to buy his farm. He wanted to become a farmer. Wanted his son to become a farmer.

Walter hedged and considered. In the end he sold his land to the baker for the value of farmland. The next year when his brother received a tax bill based on sizable development values, John understood that he could no longer afford to farm. He agreed to sell most of his land and retire. Later, they had cause to regret their decision because Sarto never farmed the land. Instead, he and his sons sold it to developers and reaped huge profits when they did so.

When Janss Corporation began its initial stages of development in Westlake Village, the event affected the family in different ways. Some were ready to leave. Some used the opportunity to sell and buy irrigated cropland in other areas of California. A few remained in the area, adjusted to the influx of new neighbors and appreciated the ease of new shopping centers. Some retained their acreage in the Conejo and sold it off, bit by bit. Tracy was among the latter.

The promise of money seemed to accomplish what bad times had not. The family became embroiled in dispute. Some members wanted to hold onto land for speculation; others wanted to sell at once. Children and grandchildren watched and listened. Relationships with each other were affected by the tensions, but we were proud that everyone stayed civil. There were misunderstandings, and later the plain talk that seems to come with old age, but the brothers and sisters remained good friends for all of their lives.

The communal well that supplied many of her sisters' domestic water was located on Tracy's portion. She was obligated to hold her land until the last of her siblings sold. This created a burden for her because after the land was reappraised from agriculture to development, her taxes soared. Our own modest five acres were reappraised from $5,000 to $50,000 an acre within a few years. Like a trim row of dominoes that had stood through four generations, once the first one fell, there was no stopping the rest.

Tracy kept her land, determined that her children should inherit as she had. Some of her sisters were much younger. Others were ready to retire. The sale of their land allowed them to live out their lives in comfort, but each retained their house and enough land to leave their children provided for. Walter Kelley signed a contract to sell his walnut trees and his flatland, except for the house and a few acres. John Kelley sold much of his the following year. Fred Kelley sold a few acres. Their sisters, Josephine and Dorothy, sold everything and moved north.

A difference of opinion erupted among the Kelleys that had always been a point of dissent. It hadn't seemed as important when the brushy hills grazed cattle in the spring and summer, but with development the issue became paramount. At the time of their grandfather Borchard's death, Josephine and Dorothy were very young. Instead of land, they were given $2,000 each, the equivalent land value at the time. Their oldest brother Charlie never married. He wrote a will that left his share to the little girls so they wouldn't be left out. A few years later the siblings re-apportioned the land to include the younger sisters in equal shares. At the time, Charlie Kelley intended to redo his will, leaving his portion to be divided among several of his nephews, but he died before it could be done. Under the terms of his existing will, his land was divided between his two adult sisters, who serendipitously ended up with a triple portion of land and money.

Some of the land amounted to brush-strewn hills worth less than the flats. Siblings paid for surveys that would apportion the hills and flatland equally to each. In spite of their efforts, not everyone was happy with the division. In the flush days of easy subdivisions, developers sought prime farmland. Those who sold in the early years did so when land prices were lower. Some of the brothers felt betrayed by Mr. Sarto when he sold to developers. Others waited years to sell. No matter how hard they tried, some were destined to benefit more than others.

Tracy and Oscar packed up their farm and moved north the year that the golf course was built along Highway 101, when housing tracts and electronics manufacturing plants began supplanting horse ranches and tomato fields. Tracy had considered her move to the Norwegian Colony a temporary one. She was sure that they would find themselves on other farmland within a few years, She ended up moving only once in her lifetime.

My parents owned a lovely five-bedroom house that had been built on the Rincon Beach area of Santa Barbara. It was located in a compound and owned by a Hollywood movie director as a summerhouse. When Highway 101 was widened, the house and the compound was condemned by the State and slated for immediate removal. My father was working at the Shell Oil refinery across the road and heard about the opportunity. He purchased a beautiful home for $1,500. He arranged to have it cut in half, loaded onto flatbed semis and trucked over Conejo Grade onto land on Borchard Road that Tracy owned. My father traded his equity as security for a loan when we purchased our new ranch property near Paso Robles, in 1959.

Tracy included the house and property in a Trust overseen by Bank of America. The house was indifferently managed, at one point lying unoccupied for over a year while vagrants lived in it. Tracy was powerless to do anything about it. When she inquired, it seemed that the bank had lost their copy of the Trust. It took over a year and a trip to Los Angeles to obtain records restoring her property.

A syndicate of investors from Los Angeles purchased my family's former house during the boom years of development. In 1964, inflated land values plummeted. A representative of the syndicate contacted Bank of America, hoping to renegotiate the terms of the purchase. When that failed they called Tracy, demanding that she renegotiate their purchase contract. Tracy would have none of it. Over the next months she received increasingly demanding letters and phone calls from their attorneys, but she held firm. A contract had been made. Who ever heard of changing the terms two years after the fact?

Later that year a suspicious fire destroyed the five-bedroom house. The investment syndicate collected on the insurance and allowed Bank of America to repossess the land.

By the late '50s, a family that had counted on each other in good times and bad began to spread out over much of California. The ties that bound us were broken. So were many hearts. In the end, Sarto and his pastries cost us far more than anyone could have estimated. When development occurred, it seemed that the family was blasted apart with the force of a nuclear explosion, particles flung to the far reaches of California. For a child it felt like the family had been reduced to pieces of sand. Separation had destroyed the thing that made us strong. We weren't connected in the same way. Cousins no longer attended the same schools; we no longer shared appreciation of the same things. We were no longer, more or less, in the same financial situation.

Of course, nothing is as dire as it seems at the time. As travel conditions improved and workloads allowed, we continued to visit each other, attended each other's weddings and funerals and held family reunions at Borchard Park. The split was more emotional than actual. People moved away, but their hearts were still connected. We learned that there are three types of trees. There are those with a taproot growing deep into the soil. Those that put down shallow roots and follow the water source wherever it flows. And those that are a combination.

Moving from the Conejo caused us to send out shallow roots. Life taught us that a deep tap root is a fine thing, but the shallow roots are the ones that nourish the tree.

Memories remain perfect only in the timeless recesses of our minds. Who but we know that in the curve of a hill beyond Kelley Road, five arrowheads were found on a September morning? Who else knows that a mountain lion sunned itself in the crotch of an oak, only minutes after four young children left it? That a rabid skunk was cornered beneath our water tank? That an asphalt driveway covers the old mink farm? That my brother, at ten, hiked to the top of Old Boney after swearing my six-year-old sister to secrecy?

I learned that time is a healing. It has taken a lifetime to understand the wounds of our leaving. As Helen Keller once said, "What we have once enjoyed deeply we can never lose. All that we love deeply becomes a part of us."

When development arrived in the Norwegian Colony, it did not come uninvited. Richard Pederson retired, married and moved to Santa Barbara. He wanted to see his property "used to provide youth the benefits of Christian Education." His donated land was eventually dedicated for use as California Lutheran University.

Rich's brothers, Pete and Lawrence, his sister Anna's estate and the Olsen brothers—Oscar and Nick—were less motivated to donate their land. They had families to consider. In a series of phone calls and letters, Cal Lutheran representatives pressed the case for adding their land to Rich's generous donation. In the end, the college purchased what they needed from Rich and his sister Anna's estate, and built a beautiful campus. Mrs. Pederson's house was moved from its original site and earthquake-proofed. It now houses the college's music department.

Oscar sold most of his land to a developer except for his own home and five and a half acres, which was eventually sold to the University. He returned once to the Conejo, intending to see what changes had occurred on his land. When he saw the eucalyptus grove, he asked that his daughter turn the car around. He never returned.

View of the bluff at the edge of the Norwegian Colony

CHAPTER EIGHTEEN

Making Cents of It

IN THE NORWEGIAN tradition, Oscar wanted to provide a farm so his son could continue to work the land. In 1957, he bought a farm in Paso Robles. As the time for them to leave grew closer, my sisters and I were gripped by a sense of loss as final as if our grandparents were leaving their homeland and sailing across the ocean—as the Norwegians had done a generation earlier. We had not visited Paso Robles, but we hated even the name. We could scarcely imagine life without the house on Olsen Road.

My sister and I were conscripted to wrap Tracy's treasures in tissue and newsprint. I worked with downcast eyes and a lump too big to swallow. Tracy seemed as devastated as we by the impending move. Her brothers and sisters were still living on the Conejo. She had wanted to stay. With bittersweet longing, my brother, sister and I stood in the granary and inhaled the scent of oats and mice, ran along the rock wall, straddled the propane tank like a horse, climbed the tank house steps, opened the Dutch doors of the playhouse that Oscar had built for his daughters. We passed from one space to another trying to absorb the sights, smells and memories. Finally, we passed the bee house, crossed the clover lawn, closed our eyes and memorized the sighing of the wind in the eucalyptus trees. We filled the car with oranges and lemons.

Their leaving felt like death. Worse than death, we were losing them and the farm at the same time. My mother was devastated. She walked the property alone, grieving in a way that I could not appreciate at the time. She asked her children to remain in the car and when she came back she couldn't speak to us. Clearly, she was fighting back tears; I understood this as a 10-year-old in a way that changed me forever. The lesson I learned that day was that *change hurts*. My life has reflected that moment. In the car my mother bit back tears. A movement interrupted her reverie; a cottontail hopped toward the hollow where the barn once stood. Apparently the rattlesnakes had left as well. When my mother slowly circled the car around the farmyard perimeter road and headed east, I thought my heart would break.

Today, Tracy's precut house is gone along with the outbuildings. The barn burned from a lightning strike and had to be dismantled. Only a few eucalyptus trees remain. When I return to visit, the Oaks Shopping Mall is half a dozen stoplights from the farm. A trip back to visit has all the elements of a class reunion—a bittersweet experience. I don't recognize any of the old gang, but I remember everything we did together.

I drove my mother on her last trip to Olsen Road. Her face reflected her memories. She gazed at the bluffs across the *Wuthering Heights* moors to the pepper tree that grew crooked because she had straddled it like a pony when it was too small to hold her. Her eyes followed the sun setting in the west, a serendipitous adieu for her final visit. Wisps of grass waved in the breeze, progeny of the seeds planted by her grandfather. Beer bottles and campfire soot disfigured the Indian caves on the hill. City teens had set fire to the eucalyptus grove and burned much of it; the trees that remained were old and failing. We tried to understand how someone could spray graffiti inside the Indian cave. We felt violated. But we realized we couldn't rage against the wind.

My words to her must have mirrored my mother's thoughts because she nodded. "For five generations, the Olsens maintained a covenant with that hill. Look what has happened. Inch by inch, they have destroyed that which we love."

———————

Oscar moved away because he would not see it developed by his own hand. It was not by accident that he returned only once before his death. The land seems broken, the swales filled by earthmovers until the contours of the land are unrecognizable. But the houses are splendid. It would be an honor to live in one of them. My mother and I agree that we are hypocrites. It is easier to blame urban sprawl than to admit that we relinquished our bond.

Modern farmers wrestle with the same issue: Development is the only way that they can recoup their losses, pay off the bank, provide for a retirement and send their children to college. They curse the city that ultimately brings high prices for land that couldn't make them a living.

An old alfalfa farmer told me that in a boom year he made enough on his farming to purchase two small lots in town. He turned around and sold them within weeks. By the time escrow closed he had made more profit on their sale than he had in his 26 years of growing alfalfa. That is a sad story, made sadder by the fact that others have made their fortunes without knowing what alfalfa is.

CHAPTER NINETEEN

Starting Over

ON DECEMBER 23, 1957, we piled into our car and drove 200 miles north to see Tracy's new house. It was the year of the hundred-year rains. We were pulled over at the Rincon by a road crew and made to wait an hour for the tide to subside as waves crashed over the seawall and flooded the Pacific Coast Highway. When the highway reopened we drove through a long stretch of saltwater and pelting rain.

We discovered a pink and white striped hamburger stand in Buellton that served malts and French fries, and we established a new family tradition. At Pismo Beach we passed a gigantic rock in the middle of the highway, our halfway point. At the Cuesta Grade we found a mountain with a seven-percent grade and a harrowing view of deep ravines. In the rain it seemed even steeper than the Norwegian Grade. At Paso Robles we found a quiet town with wide streets and a beautiful city park. And we began to hope.

The Olsen Ranch sign greeted us from a welded pipe near Oscar's new mailbox at the entrance to the driveway. The sign had been carried from the old farm, formed years earlier by someone pounding strap steel on an anvil. We started down the driveway and with our first glance we were prepared to forgive our grandparents for moving. The house was grand. It overlooked the fields from a height of two stories with a dark, forbidding basement that could only be reached by wickedly narrow concrete steps. It was perfect. A huge antique wood-burning cookstove stood in the long back porch beside a table that could hold 14 farmhands.

The farm shop had a dirt floor that smelled of diesel, just like Oscar's old one. We discovered a pair of bunkhouses, freshly swept, with tiny shower stalls and metal beds with creaky springs and well-worn mattresses. Showers were new to us. We were accustomed to clawfoot bathtubs. We crossed a narrow footbridge spanning a running creek and entered a dairy barn with concrete floors redolent of stale cow manure. Sheep we were accustomed to, but the abandoned production line of a dairy was a daring move for our grandfather to have made.

Tracy had become friends with Les and Jenny Ericson, the farmers who sold the place. Their children's names were etched in concrete at the corner of the patio. We met Jenny at church on Sunday and her sad Italian smile told me all that I needed to know. It had not been by choice that they had left their farm.

The house was painted with thick layers of oil-based enamel. From the looks of it, even the paint had an air of permanence. Tracy's new house was designed with cubbies and built-in shelves. Arched doorways connected the rooms. A fireplace held a fire with huge oak logs. Oscar's books and magazines already filled a pair of bookcases. In each bedroom, built-in cabinets, desks and linen closets covered an entire wall. Each second story window had a view of the farm.

The next summer it would become the aunts' project to wallpaper the upper bedrooms. While the cousins played in the lawn sprinklers, my mother and her sisters gossiped and put up Alberta peaches, papered and painted, rearranged furniture and worked in Tracy's vegetable garden.

The barn dwarfed the outbuildings. Oscar's hay pulley already hung above stacks of alfalfa bales in the tall, tin-roofed hay barn. The sweet, musty scent of dried alfalfa was new to us. Instead of eucalyptus, this ranch had Valley Oaks dripping with mistletoe and Spanish moss, a reservoir for swimming and woodlands perfect for hunting Easter eggs. Our mothers seemed equally enchanted. Months earlier they had choked back their tears and tried to make peace with their parent's move. Now they could be happy.

It was our mothers who found the way to differentiate between the farms. The first was forever to be called "The Home Place." The second was simply, "Grandpa's Farm." When Neil took over the farming, we had less reason to venture out to the fields so it ceased to be a farm and became simply "Grandma's House," where Tracy served cookies and tea.

Tracy and Oscar lived out their lives in the farmhouse, shaded from the California sun by a half-dozen mature cottonwood trees. Their lives seem idyllic in today's world, but they would not claim theirs had been perfect. Oscar was especially hard on his son. He and Neil argued over Neil's agricultural college farming methods, which seemed to contradict Oscar's own hard-earned wisdom. Stubborn and quiet, Oscar maintained the habits of a first-generation American. On reflection, he wouldn't have thought his life remarkable. He simply lived a day at a time, doing what needed to be done. Oscar had a solid, plodding gait about him for all the years that I knew him. The tubes of Ben Gay on his nightstand hinted at years of chronic pain from worn-out joints and a bad heart, but he never complained.

In the final two years that followed his stroke, he kept vigil in a recliner near the fire and watched his family with joy in his faded blue eyes. He was silent then, unable to speak, his shock of white hair folded across his wide forehead, the band of farmer tan gone from his hairline. But his smile remained; a crinkly lifting of appreciation at the full glass that life had brought him. On my visit to his deathbed he motioned to one of his daughters to fetch me to his side. I was so touched. Somehow I had expected that the roomful of wife and daughters would be enough for him, but he grasped my hand when I bent to brush my lips across the white stubble of his cheek. Such a simple gesture, but not simple at all.

I think of Grandpa and Grandma often, when the wind teases the young branches of the redwoods I planted in their honor. Not sycamores, for they are too thirsty. Not cottonwoods, for they are messy, each spring, exuding basketsful of cottony hairs that cover the ground and blow into the open doorway. Like the dusty blue gum eucalyptus that Lars Pederson and Nils Olsen planted for firewood, there are better varieties. The old ways have passed, but not the scrape of limb on roof. That sound is eternal.

CHAPTER TWENTY

Reflections

STILLNESS INTEGRATED MY grandfather's parts and rendered him complete. Like farmers everywhere, Oscar needed solitude to allow his reasoning and logic. Whenever confounded, he would walk the hills or the sheep paths. In the quietness of nature his mind blotted out the confusion of modern life. When angered he would leave the room and work among his animals or his machinery until his nerves calmed. He carried his opinions until he saw a reason to change, which could be years. An idea once inside his head would remain there. There is a saying about "stubborn Swedes." He showed that it goes the same for Norwegians.

Oscar could forgive the sinner, but never the sin. In his purest form, the silence of falling dusk was to his soul what the ring of a cash register is to a merchant. Silence served as a reminder that life is good. He controlled his fears with his own labor. Curious and willing to learn, he took side jobs that allowed him to farm his land until his crops were ready. Oscar saved to buy one of the first tractors in the Conejo and traveled to Los Angeles to learn how to repair it. He served on a murder trial and didn't talk about it. He watched six siblings die and didn't cry until he saw their coffins, sixty years later.

For him time was a commodity, like cash. He wasted neither. And he understood that a good wife was essential to his success. Women worked side-by-side, as did Karn Pederson on the Norwegian Colony, when she raised her children with her husband's memory to guide her, or spent her waking hours helping to sand and candle thousands of eggs a day in the solitude of a little egg house. Or Lina Hanson, who farmed her husband's land while he lay in bed for a year. Part of each partner's commitment included resisting the urge to complain, even when disaster followed disaster.

For the farmer's wife, solitude often carried a steeper price. When the Norwegians blasted a road that connected them to the railroad, it came too late for the wives whose husbands died of undiagnosed disease, or for those whose children died without access to a hospital.

From childhood, I observed that the farmers of my acquaintance seemed not opposed to conversation so much as satisfied with the good, natural conversations that they carried on inside their heads during a lifetime of solitary labor. A gregarious farmer might talk to his dogs, or for a lack of other companionship, to his sheep and milk cow. If every farmer was like my grandfather, he needed his space. By the end of the day he had settled his conflicts. He could return to the house with no need to speak of matters that troubled him. When he gathered with other farmers, conversation was often in the form of information gathering and exchange. He would process later, when solitude afforded the opportunity.

When a man like Lud Olsen stopped farming and moved to town because neither he nor his wife could tolerate the remoteness of the Colony, he thrived among social people and he followed his heart. The land was our heritage, a bond to the past, but it did not limit us. Only our regrets can do that.

A generation later, many of us have taken jobs that reflect our farm roots. Others were fortunate enough to inherit land from their parents and continue farming with an unbroken seam. Before they took over control of their family farms, many earned a degree from an agricultural college. Today, college is an essential part of agriculture. Sons come home from college and argue progressive methods with their fathers. Their success will be more elusive than it was for our great-grandfathers, who lived in the brief period of American farming when land was cheap, labor was plentiful, and a burgeoning population paid well for crops that could not be shipped long distances. Men made use of apprenticeship, common sense and shared knowledge. Their great-grandsons use computers, accountants and genetic technology. If they could have a conversation with the old men of the Conejo, the old farmers would undoubtedly hold their own.

The sound of argument still stirs the evening breeze along many rural roads. If one hears voices of old farmers raised in passionate discourse, it might be brothers gathered around a farmhouse dinner table. The luxury of being able to strongly disagree belongs to families who know each other well.

Our ancestors might approve of our flocking to the cities to earn university credentials, but they might be disappointed in our children's lack of common sense. Farm children find themselves in a society that seems to no longer value tradition. Education has become increasingly theory-based as our society delegates more of its resources to decisions by committee and consensus building. Right and wrong are relative; moral values that must be weighed and applied appropriately. Kids believe the things they are taught in school. They are becoming socialists.

––––––––––

By the 1880s, the fertile farm valleys of California had filled with farmers. Thirty-some years after American laws stripped native-born Californians of their land grants, after the "'49ers" gave up and the gold rush settled down, the land was ripe for farming. San Diego, Santa Barbara and San Francisco were thriving sea towns. A few men became millionaires when they built railroads with public money and cheap Chinese labor—arteries that opened up California's interior valleys to farmers.

It had been Jose de la Guerra's fortune to count the Rancho El Conejo among his holdings. Although he was an aggressive rancher and trader, de la Guerra was no farmer. During his stewardship the land remained untilled. Through a series of events dictated by bankers, investors, speculators, politicians—and nature in the form of droughts and floods—the land changed hands once, twice and once again. The arrival of determined European immigrants on the southeastern edge of Ventura County pressed plow to furrow, field to barley and bean. Earlier arrivals purchased the land for $2-$3 an acre, from land brokers who knew a good thing when they saw it. Later arrivals like Caspar Borchard Sr. paid a little over $6 per acre for the same land, after bankers and drought wore the edges from the original pioneers.

It was a time of cheap land, of horse and man-power where each depended on the other. It was a time when life expectancy was low, owing to accidents and illnesses. Family histories record children dying from a cold caught while swimming on a cool day, from a panther's mauling and from tuberculosis. My grandfather was one of three children in his family to live to adulthood when six others died in childhood. Is it any wonder that family photographs show mothers solemn-faced and stoic; fathers worn and bent? People wore out. The pragmatism that created a rural network in the Conejo Valley differed little from that of other areas. More than simply the story of the Conejo, this is the story of a thousand valleys.

I was born at the end of an era. I watched my vast, extended family fuss and rally, celebrate and render mutual aid. I never questioned that my world view was normal and reasonable. Nor do I now. But by every standard that I apply, it seems as though society has lost more than it has gained since the middle of the Twentieth Century. Communities hold parades and build museums and interpretive centers. We don pioneer garb and give spinning and churning demonstrations to school children, but we are enacting a memory. For the most part, the pragmatism and grit of America is gone, and we are only pretending when we say that it is not.

So what remains? Is it only our memories and those twists in the loops of our DNA, those odd ways of thinking and behaving that set us apart from the rest of society as the last generation of farm children-turned-urban? Some of us have trouble fitting into a culture where polished and poised are the new hallmarks, where plain speech and bull-headedness create social discord. Still too close to the old ways, we see little reason to trade our values for others that might seem artificially slick and calculated. We accept progress with a sigh; pick and choose what we will embrace.

We are the last generation to be reared under the expectation that hard work will be rewarded. We have watched men without calluses become billionaires in an electronic age, and we feel betrayed. We are the men and women raising sheep and cattle on our five acre suburban plots while we work full-time jobs in town. We grow peaches and apples, and spend our weekends canning them into Mason jars before returning to jobs that pay our bills. We can't understand why our children won't help in the family garden, why our children and grandchildren have rejected our belief in hard work and have replaced it with confidence in a New World Economy. Our advice, our religion, our way of life seems to have become archaic. We are becoming a service economy where no one wants to be the servant.

Our children think we are dinosaurs, fools for our work ethic and our slavish devotion to the old ways, and maybe we are. We seem to be caught in a schizophrenic blur between the old and the new. We distrust bio-engineered food and altered milk. We remember when things tasted real. Many of us can still milk a cow. We recall our grandmother's roses and geraniums before the nursery industry hybridized nature and the scent of flowers disappeared in a concession to a longer "sell-by" date

180

and climate change. We recall when trees were planted in both male and female varieties, the females making a mess in the yards with their pods and debris. But they attracted the pollen that now floats uselessly in the air. Now we sneeze and give allergy medicines to medicate our children's asthma. We drink our pasteurized milk because we gave up the fight to find raw. But we remember that the old ways were healthier.

We study photographs of our ancestors and we notice that hardly anyone was fat. We remember the '50s, when sodas, flavored drink mixes, white bread and potato chips came into our diets, when sugar became synonymous with a mother's love. We remember school prayer, spankings, being sent outside to play on stick horses and having to change into play clothes. We remember twice a week baths and saying "thank-you". And calling our parent's friends by Mr. and Mrs. instead of by their first names.

Now we are hounded by the guilt of our abandonment. Things are out of kilter and we suspect that we are to blame. Our grandparents' photographs remind us that we forgot their lessons along the way. They were disciplined in a way that we are not; focused in a way that we have lost. True, theirs was a world of fewer choices. I doubt, given the nature of our temptations, that they would have done any better. But the fact is, we failed to heed their maxim: *Waste not, want not.* Now we must brace ourselves for the consequences.

We are tied to the thinking that formed our values. From a farmer's viewpoint, when a man moves away from his farm and takes a job in town, he has lost his stillness. He feels trapped. The baying of a neighbor's dog or the screeching of tires becomes almost unbearable cacophony. The city puts off unnatural heat that emanates from the concrete, from steam vents and even from the crush of human bodies. Skyscrapers create unnatural canyons closed to cooling breezes. Like a wildfire, the city creates its own climate. Airborne particles cling to the skin and suffocate the pores. Water tastes metallic, and of chlorine. It runs tepid from the tap, not chilled from the recesses of the earth.

We daughters of the soil sprung from our own roots in different directions. Some of us flocked to town and thrived; donned high heels and long, lacquered nails and took jobs as secretaries. Others see themselves as partners with husbands or brothers in the hallowed tradition of the West. This being the case, we drive a pick-up truck and a tractor with equal enthusiasm, count a new pair of Wranglers as our spring wardrobe and greet any man as a friend and peer. Yet we seem caught in the middle, unsure where we belong. We work at town jobs, but drive a tractor on Saturday mornings. We daydream of satin robes and vacations to far-away places. We help castrate sheep, but wear gloves to protect our nail polish. Some of us marry city boys and spend our lives trying to figure out why some of their ways make us act so cantankerous.

Is the farmer's or stockman's view a romantic one? Undoubtedly. Is it fair? Maybe not. Maybe the issue of fairness is beside the point. Like nationalism or patriotism, we agrarians cling to a set of values that define our being.

One of the benefits of living in a family enclave was the opportunity to observe our kin. When a child watches his grandfather experiment with crop rotation and animal husbandry, he learns the lessons for a lifetime. Schoolbooks would have us believe that there are no social lines in America, just as there are no racial lines, but we know better. Since peasants began clustering crofts together to create towns, since sea trade and specialization necessitated a cash economy, we have had a farmer class. Rita Mae Brown, in her book, *Starting from Scratch*, penned it well. For the English-speaking, the situation was made serious in 1066, when Harold fell at Hastings, shot through the eye with an arrow. Since the Normans overwhelmed the Anglo-Saxons and hybridized our language with French, we have had "farmer English" and "city English", called in its proper form, "high" English and "low" English.

High English is Latinesque, grand and expressive. We use it to describe culture and enjoyment of life. If a Norman nobleman sat to eat, he dined. He ate beef while the farmer/serf raised oxen. Meat served at table was venison, from the deer that grazed outside. Lords dined on pork; farmers raised pigs. The same for fowl and chicken, lamb and mutton. The list continues. Farmers kept their language when they died, helped, dressed, worked and were happy. Should someone wish to gain acceptance into urban or court society, they replaced these simple words with perish, aided, clothed, toiled and experienced felicity. The farmer continued to use the low form and was often thought a dullard when judged alongside his city cousin. Those of us who knew our farmer grandparents realize that this was not so. When the noblest of Lords fell into a swill, he hollered "Help!" not "Aid!" (Our grandfathers understood that providing aid to the needy seldom provided a permanent solution.) Word choices learned from immigrant teachers have afforded a lifetime of opportunities to improve our station in life.

To watch a farmer fashion a tractor part on his lathe, or weld a broken implement, is to watch an engineer at work. To sit around a table and hear farmers argue politics, economics and social policy is to attend a grass-roots university. The lessons go on, day and night, for those of us who listen. Economic factors may conspire against the family farmer. A cash economy may favor the urbanite, but the farmer should feel no shame. Although the farmer may envy the coins jingling in the pockets of his city brother, the farmer does not begrudge him. Rather he is frustrated because mega dollars, not brawn or stubbornness, now define success.

In the early days of farming, ownership of land defined a man's worth. A man with many sons and daughters, much land and many horses had little need of cash except to buy staples and to pay his taxes. His grain seed was hearty. He could save a portion in reserve to plant in the fall. The land was verdant and fertile. Fertilizers and sprays were not needed. Horsepower was cheaply fed on hay and grain from the farmer's own field. When tractors arrived, the farmer fared even better. He increased his tillage. Eggs and butter paid for his staples. Flour sacks provided cloth for his children's garments until they started school. Women and girls grew gardens and sewed the family's clothing.

Careful stewardship is synonymous with farming—an image both wholesome and heartening, even if it isn't always true. But as farmers, we believe in the concept. We believe that our countrymen can rest easy, knowing that the farmer is upholding the tenets that made America great. We resist efforts by outsiders who tell us how to manage our livestock, our water run-off and the wolves that attack our cattle. We see ourselves as stewards of the land and mutter that big city environmentalists should mind their own business. Like it or not, we feel that grazing our herds on public land prevents fire danger, that wild horses are a nuisance, and that the .22 rifle is God's way of keeping the varmint population in check. We maintain a deep distrust of government, we love our children and their sports, and we wish that city slickers would not create a ranchette subdivision down the road or burn our fields with their cigarettes. We can recite the Pledge of Allegiance and the Lord's Prayer, and do so at every opportunity. We eat beef and don't plan to die of artery disease.

WW II brought mass consumerism, and with it an end to institutionalized frugality. Farmers left the farm and learned that impulse was a lot more fun than saving for a rainy day. Television brought a world of consumer goods and places to visit. Farmers learned that they liked to travel. Increasingly, they lacked the cash to indulge in their wants and needs while public money favored the emerging classes of landless poor. Farmers couldn't compete in a cash economy and they couldn't qualify for assistance, even if they wanted to. When the farmer's children clamored to attend college, they discovered that land-poor farmers owned too many assets for their children to qualify for grants or scholarships. Applications had to be turned in by January 31, too early for farmers to compute their expenses of the precious year and file their tax return. Under existing rules, their children didn't qualify for government loans. Everywhere we turned, society counted on the farmer to feed the nation and the world cheaply, while merchants and futures traders made fortunes selling goods and services that raised the farmer's cost of doing business.

By 1959, the cycle caught up with us. Victor Davis Hanson, in his book, *The Land was Everything*, writes that only decades ago, a 20 pound box of plums sold for four dollars. Today, the shopper takes them home from the supermarket for $1.99 a pound—and the farmer makes the same profit as he did back then. Worse, the farmer's income arrives in seasonal increments, much of it in mid or late summer, while his expenses continue year-around. Instead of dancing all night at a harvest celebration like his great-grandfathers, the modern farmer is more likely to sit at the kitchen table with his wife and juggle unpaid bills.

A similar gulf divides stockman and farmer. Stockmen raise cattle and horses, trusting on the rains to keep the ravines and canyons fortified with nourishing grass. Many of them feel like the farmer is crazy to struggle against nature. Why, they ask, put all that work into breaking the ground? Why not sit back and let cattle do what they do best—eat? In contrast, the farmer values his own physical labor. He often considers the stockman lazy.

I understand the argument both ways.

A stockman cousin remarked to me once at a family gathering, how hard my father had worked us on the farm. I found myself wanting to respond, "What else were we supposed to do with our time?" but I held my tongue. Intellectually, I know the answer. I have been to Paris, to university and have found pleasure in a number of avocations, but for a moment my core beliefs clamored to be heard. To a farmer, hard physical work is so fine a discipline, leaves a body so sated at the end of a day, that the ache of a day's labor is the feeling of being alive. Even when forced to drop off my high school tennis team because I was needed in the fields after school, I understood my father's reasoning. My disappointment was a trade-off. My value to my family was a matter of survival. To a kid, that was a heady responsibility.

The enmity between farmer and city dweller has been stoked by the commercialism that convinces us that we need all things, regardless of our ability to pay for them. The farm wife is characterized as thrifty, comfortable in a worn-out dress without a blush of self-consciousness. This isn't true now and probably never was. The truth is, a farmer's wife doesn't indulge herself in recreational shopping trips to the mall. She doesn't allow herself to visit Macy's until the last week of their seasonal sale—and then she justifies her purchases as layaway birthday gifts. Sometimes the homemade jams and butter-light cinnamon rolls she gives for Christmas may seem a little provincial, even to her.

So the farmer continues to farm with one eye on the encroaching city. By the time it arrives he has experienced the accompanying rise in property taxes, has fended off a half-dozen realtors and knows to the penny what his land is worth. The irony of the situation is not lost on most farmers. They face complicated formulas of how and whether to sell. Some of their sons want to remain on the land. Some do not. They keep an eye on inheritance tax laws and calculate their net worth. They tally the costs of retirement against the fear of sitting out their last days on the Home Place, trying to stay out of their children's hair.

Some secretly hope that a developer will offer them big bucks for their property and they can sell for many times the land's value while their neighbors continue to farm and maintain the rural atmosphere. It is not only Los Angelenos fleeing to a retirement paradise that want to close the gate behind them. The farmer is often guilty of the same.

This is the reality of farming in California today. This was the case in the Conejo Valley in 1957, when development exploded with the intensity of a bomb. Within a couple of years it seemed as though the entire valley floor had been covered in houses, streets and shopping centers.

Joe Russell Sr., a pioneer son whose father established the Russell Ranch in what is now Westlake Village, wrote his impressions of the valley into two volumes, *Cattle on the Conejo*, and later, *Heads and Tails. . . and Odds and Ends*. He said it for all of us in his understatement: "Those of us who have lived in El Conejo and Ventura County all our lives are a little surprised, and even a little bewildered, at what has happened to us in the space of a few short years."

As a wave of newcomers entered the floodgates and initiated a new era, another gate opened at the other end of the valley by which the farmers and ranchers quietly left.

Since writing the original manuscript nearly twenty years ago—and after moving to Southern Oregon—I've witnessed a renaissance in people returning to the land. Young people are creating truck farms, selling produce at farmer's markets and farm stands. Young brewers and vintners are resurging. Farm-to-Table restaurants support local farmers. Diners appreciate the added value by paying more for locally sourced food. Raised garden beds and goat mulch fill up backyards. Society is shifting values to support what we feel is important. The younger generation is leading us back to nature.

Chapter Twenty-one

Branches

Borchard Family

CASPAR BORCHARD SR. (purchased farmland in the Conejo in 1882.)

Wife: THERESA MARING BORCHARD (Born in Andover, Germany. Died of stomach cancer.)

ROSA (My great-grandmother. Married Silas Fields Kelley. Farmed the Conejo.)

MARY (Raised her siblings after her mother's death. Farmed in the Conejo.)

LEO (Married Marie Hauptman. No children. Farmed in Orange County.)

CASPAR JR. (Married Ida Ayala. Children: Milton, Helen, Maryann, Fay and Jimmy. Farmed in the Conejo. Carved the oak table.)

ANTONE (Married Anna Kellner. Children: Vincent, Frances, Bernice, Wilma, Anita. Farmed in Orange County. Imported Percheron stallions.)

FRANK (Married Myrtle Heaston. Children: Alice, Alfred, Barbara. Feedlot in Imperial.)

CHARLES (Married Caroline Haidu. Children: Elizabeth, Charles, Caroline, Richard, Jack, Paul. Farmed in Orange County.)

TERESA (Married Edward V. Borchard. Children: Margaret, Edward, Robert, Rita, Alan. Formed Borchard Brothers Ranch with sons.)

Caspar Sr.'s and Theresa's relatives:

BROTHER JOHN (Purchased land in Oxnard Caspar had been renting after he was delayed in Germany.)

UNCLE CHRISTIAN (First to arrive. Farmed in Antioch upon arrival. Farme*d.*)

COUSINS FREDRICHS (Farmed opposite side of Newbury Park and Oxnard.)

Kelley Family

(First lived in Los Angeles area. Purchased property from Caspar Borchard in 1888.)

JOHN REILY KELLEY (Married Mildred Pearce. Widowed, brought family by wagon train from Nebraska. Known for owning a big black stallion.)

JOHN REILY JR. (Married Lucy Finch. Traveled from California to Texas by wagon train with their 10 children. After his death she would visit. Her best dress was black beaded dress from times past.)

THEADORE (Married Mary Mallory. 10 children. Lived in Los Angeles area.)

OLIVER (Married Nellie. 6 children. Lived in San Fernando.)

JAMES NEWTON

ANTONIE

MELISSA (Married Joe Buchard. 2 children. Cowboy husband went to look for work and was never heard from again. She then married Ed Hunter, lived in Arizona.)

ELIZABETH "LIZZY" (Married Warren Walker. No children. lived in Arizona and Ventu Park. Ranch cook for Caspar Borchard Jr.)

SILAS (Married my great-grandmother Rosa Borchard.)

CHARLIE (A bachelor. Lived with his widowed mother until his death from a heart attack at 49.)

THERESA "TRACY" (My grandmother. Married Oscar Olsen. Had 5 children and lived in Conejo Valley.)

JOHN (Married Olive "Babe" Smith. Lived in Thousand Oaks and Newbury Park.)

> CATHERINE (Married John Moragne. 2 children. Lived New York and Texas. Catherine was teacher, John an oil co. executive.)

> JOHN JR. (Married Alta Thurman. Had 3 children. Lived Newbury Park and Valley Springs. John became partially paralyzed from horse accident.)

> MICHAEL (Married Merrie Lester. Had 2 children. Live in Camarillo. Both Veterinarians at their own practice, Cottage Hospital in Oxnard.)

WALTER (Married Helga Paulson, no children. Ran dairy and later grew walnuts in Newbury Park.)

FREDRICK (Married Mildred Haynes. Had 4 children. Fred a Fire Chief at Port Hueneme.)

> FRED JR. (Married Joyce Spurlock. Had 3 children. Fred retired space engineer. Lived on original Kelley property.)

> WILLIAM "BILL" (Married Madeline Ayala. Had 5 children. Lives in Newbury Park. Bill later married Diane.)

> ROBERT "BOBBY" (Married Betty Brossard. Had 2 children. Lived in Newbury Park.)

> PATRICIA (Married William Pickering. Had 2 children Lived in Grover City.)

ROSE (Married Harry Fletcher. Had 3 children. Lived in Thousand Oaks. Died at 36 of breast cancer.)

> RALPH (Married Joan Purdy. Had 4 children. Later married Jane Purdy. Lived in Grass Valley)

> DONNIE (Killed by panther. Buried on third birthday.)

> PATRICK (Married Judith Garrett. Had 2 children. Lived Grass Valley. Was a baby when his mother died.)

DOROTHY (Married Earl Ashby. Ran a beauty shop near the Lion Farm until her marriage. Earl was a career Navy man.)

EARL JR. "JUNEY" (Had 1 child, Tana. Later married Karen Thomas. Died 2020 in Washington State.)

JILL (Married Charlie Warren and Bill Skaggs. Had 3 girls.)

JOSEPHINE (Married Cyril Colwell. Both worked at Camarillo State Hospital.)

JACQUELINE (Married James Stone. Had 8 children. Lived in South Lake Tahoe.)

DONNA (Married Aubrey McGreagor. Had 4 children. Lived in South Lake Tahoe.)

VICKIE (Married Robert Gouin. Had 3 children. Lives in Paso Robles.)

LULU (Nothing known.)

EMMIE "MINNIE" (Married Tomas Andrews. Had 3 children. Lived in Fresno and Globe, Arizona. Wore cast-off, formal black taffeta dresses regardless of the weather. Inherited Lizzy's house in Ventu Park.)

Olsen Family

NILS OLSEN: (Born Nils Uren. Married Ellen Fjorstad. Changed name to Olsen when he purchased property.)

ELLEN PETRINE IVERSDATTER FJORSTAD (changed to Iverson. Died May, 1923.)

PAULA died at 1 month.

NORA died at age 5 years.

OSCAR (Married Theresa "Tracy" Kelley. Lived on Olsen Road until 1957 when they moved to Paso Robles.)

ARTHELIA (Married Alloys "Jack" Honerkamp. Lived in Moorpark and Whittier. Children Helen, Larry, Vincent, Rosemary.)

Eugenia "Jean" (Married Wilbur Thompson. Lived in Moorpark, Newbury Park, Shandon and Paso Robles. Children: Melvin, Teresa Ann, Martha, Joan, Matthew Paul, Brian and Laura.)

Mary (Married Earl Rydberg, widower with 5 children, namely Suzanne, Peter, Jeffrey, Gail and Sharon. Mary and Earl's children: Frank, Daniel, Rose Anna, Kathleen and James. Lived on Olsen Road and Oxnard.)

Neil (Married Gisela Fritchle. Lived on their farm in Paso Robles. Children: Bernard, Ingrid and Eric.)

Emma died at age 7 years.

Ludwig (Married Hazel Mundel, no children. Then married Irene McAfee who had a son, Robert by a previous marriage. Lived in Santa Barbara.)

Nora died at age 4 years.

Laura died at age 7 years.

Ned died at age 8 years.

Thora died at age 7 years.

Niclolas "Nick" (Married Sarah Davis. Remained on the Norwegian Colony until his death. Built the miniature stagecoach displayed at the Stagecoach Inn. Sarah was a homemaker, later Psychiatric Supervisor at Camarillo State Hospital. Nick taught Woodworking at CSH.)

Gerald "Gerry" (Married Joan Turner. Had 2 children. Retired Public Information Officer for Moorpark College. Lives in Camarillo.)

Jeanette (Married Tony Franklin. Had 2 children, Lived in Redding.)

Jeanne (Married Eddie Franklin. Have 5 children. Lives in Thousand Oaks.)

David (Married Delores Bernich. Have 2 children. Lives in Simi.)

The Norwegian Colony

OLE ANDERSON: Never farmed Lot 1. Returned to Norway. His land was later purchased by Nils Olsen and became Oscar and Theresa's farm when they married.

LARS AND KARN PEDERSON: Farmed Lot 2. Died 1901. Karn and family, Pete, Rich, Anna and Lawrence moved to Santa Barbara. Boys returned to farm the Conejo until retirement. Some of their land was donated to California Lutheran University.

OLE AND ELIZABETH NELSON farmed Lot 3. Moved to northern California during a drought. Elizabeth was Lars Pederson's sister.

JORGEN AND LINA HANSEN farmed Lot 4. After Jorgen's death, Lina and her daughter returned to Norway.

NILS AND ELLEN OLSEN farmed Lot 5 until 1914 when they moved to Moorpark for Ellen's health. Oscar and Ludwick stayed and farmed their property on the Conejo. Later, Nicolas farmed as well.

About the Author

Anne is a descendant of one of the Norwegian Colony families. A fifth generation Californian, her love of the West was fueled by stories of bandits and hangings, of the stories recreated in this book, of Indian caves and of women who made their own way.

She earned a B.S. in Social Science from Cal Poly State University, SLO. Her first job was waitressing at a truck-stop cafe in Cholame, near the spot where James Dean died.

Anne is past-President of Women Writing the West. She lives in Southern Oregon with her husband, two Labs and several free-range chickens. She is a proud grandmother of two. Her interests include: reading, discovering new historical sites, hiking the Pacific Northwest trails and hearing from readers.

Blog: http://anneschroederauthor.blogspot.com/

Facebook: www.facebook.com/anneschroederauthor

Website: www.anneschroederauthor.com

Email: info@anneschroederauthor.com

If you enjoyed this book, consider leaving a review on Amazon, Goodreads, Bookbub or your own social media.

Other Books by Anne Schroeder

Memoir

Branches on the Conejo
ISBN: 1891954-99-7

Winner, William Sayoran Persie Award for Non-Fiction

No Longer in Print (RD&C Publishing)

"Anne Schroeder draws a detailed picture of the first farming families who settled in the Conejo Valley overlapping the 19th and 20th centuries…She successfully describes the interdependence of the varied heritages that came together to build a strong community."

– Amazon 5-Star Review

Ordinary Aphrodite

"*Ordinary Aphrodite* literally offered my sense of being a woman in this world a wonderful tune-up! I found myself placing penciled checkmarks beside those passages that rang my chimes, that resonated within me in a kindred-spirit kind of way. Anne's book of essays about her life is now more than a favorite. Her memoir is a keeper."

— Amazon 5-Star Review

HISTORICAL NOVELS

The Central Coast Series

Maria Ines

Finalist, Will Rogers Medallion Award, Western Inspirational Fiction

ISBN: 978-1-4328-3277-3   Five Star Publishing

"This accurate and well-researched historical fiction pulls you in to a past world not frequently explored, delivering an eye-opening account of what women endured during this dark time. It's a tale of one woman's strength and fortitude as she fought to live and love amidst death and desolation. Truly inspirational."

— Amazon 5-Star

Cholama Moon

Named "Best Non-Traditional Western Novel,"
Stu Rosebrook, *True West Magazine*

https://www.amazon.com/dp/B07JCLDHSH/
ISBN: 9781725606913

"Anne Schroeder writes a story that is not only great, she write with amazing detail. When you are reading one of her books, you feel as if you are watching a movie. In fact I would love it if this was a movie!"

– Amazon 5-Star Review

The Caballero's Son
(Fall 2021, Five Star Press)

A love story in the tradition of Helen Hunt Jackson's *Ramona*. This stand-alone novel, the third in the Central Coast Series, follows Miguelito's tumultuous life from the time his mother Maria Ines, sends him away to safety. A mother's love has no bounds, nor a son's sense of betrayal."

– Beta Reader Review

Norske Fields

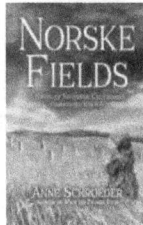

A true-life novel of Southern California's Norwegian Colony Can a handful of Norwegian immigrants build a legacy for their children in a land of bright horizons and the unforgiving earth?

ISBN: 978-1-7348684-0-1 October, 2020. Amazon, B&N, Kindle

Western Historical Romance

Walk the Promise Road

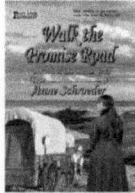

Winner 2019 Will Rogers Medallion Award for Western Romance

https://www.amazon.com/dp/B07C7H5WP8

Prairie Rose Publishing

"The history and detail is some of the best I've ever read about the Oregon Trail. Engaging characters make this hard to put down. I've been a fan of Oregon Trail stories my whole life, and this book definitely is at the top of my all time favorites list."
                                                              — Amazon 5-Star Review

Boy in the Darkness

Shortlisted, 2020 Will Rogers Award for Western Short Fiction

https://www.amazon.com/dp/B07SV52KPN

Trailblazer Western Fiction

"His struggle to survive occupies his mind, body and spirit with surprising results. A hundred and fifty years later the echoes of his struggle remain when a Lakota Indian advisor finds signs of his passage in the limestone cave."
                                                              — Amazon 5-Star Review

Short Stories

Gifts of Red Pottery

https://www.amazon.com/dp/1976467977

"A collection of emotion stirring short stories gathered together from her many years of writing and given as a gift to her readers. Men and women alike will be touched by her stories—current and past, dark ones and light ones, tough and gentle; each tale a stand-alone gem."

– Amazon 5-Star Review